GET YOUR MESSAGE ACROSS

GET YOUR MESSAGE ACROSS

The professional communication skills everyone needs

Jacqui Ewart
Gail Sedorkin
Tony Schirato

ALLEN & UNWIN

First published in 1998 by
Allen & Unwin
9 Atchison Street
St Leonards NSW 1590
Australia
Phone: (61 2) 8425 0100
Fax: (61 2) 9906 2218
E-mail: frontdesk@allen-unwin.com.au
Web: http://www.allen-unwin.com.au

National Library of Australia
Cataloguing-in-Publication entry:

Ewart, Jacqui.
   Get your message across: the professional communication
   skills everyone needs.

   Includes index.
   ISBN 1 86448 670 8.

   1. Communication—Handbooks, manuals, etc. 2. Public
   relations—Handbooks, manuals, etc. 3. Publicity—
   Handbooks, manuals, etc. I. Sedorkin, Gail. II. Schirato,
   Anthony. III. Title.

302.2

Set in 10/12 pt Garamond by DOCUPRO, Sydney

Printed by Alken Press, Sydney

10 9 8 7 6 5 4 3 2

Contents

About the authors

JACQUI EWART is a lecturer in journalism and professional communication at Central Queensland University. She recently completed her Master of Arts in Aboriginal Studies, and will soon start a PhD in journalism.

GAIL SEDORKIN is a journalism and professional communication lecturer at Central Queensland University, combining her two loves of journalism and teaching. Her research work has covered such areas as travel writing and interviewing.

TONY SCHIRATO lectures in the Department of Communication and Media Studies at Central Queensland University. He is co-author, with Susan Yell, of *Communication and Cultural Literacies* (Allen & Unwin 1996).

Acknowledgements

JACQUI EWART

I would like to thank my soul mate Peter Savill for his listening ear and unfailing support. Thanks also to my parents Jack and Pauline Ewart, especially you Dad for encouraging me to read and write for all those years and for your suggestions for titles.

GAIL SEDORKIN

Special thanks firstly to Kev Kavanagh and Fran Moore of *The Cairns Post* newspaper for their professional advice and input. I would particularly like to thank my husband, Nick, and my parents, Lou and Mollie Svanetti, for all their help and support along the way, and also my sister, Lisa, and brother, Andrew.

TONY SCHIRATO

Thanks to Jeanette Delamoir, April Harwood, Peter Lawrence, Errol Veith and Susan Yell at Central Queensland University, and Elizabeth Weiss, Christa Munns and the staff at Allen & Unwin for their assistance.

Introduction

Have you ever been asked to write something urgently, only to find yourself at a complete loss as to how to start? Do you know how to write a press release or prepare an urgent briefing note? Can you help your boss prepare a speech? Whether you work in public relations, marketing, or in some other part of an organisation, you probably need to prepare and disseminate information. If you are a professional communicator, or even if communication is just one part of your job, this book provides you with the answers to these and other questions. It will help you to develop the skills and expertise that you will need to prepare a range of communication material and events.

Knowing what to say, how to say it, to whom you are saying it and the best way of getting that information to your audience is vital in today's information world, where a smorgasbord of written and visual information is available. This book introduces you to a variety of communication formats, both written and verbal, as well as methods for organising and presenting information. Most importantly, it will help you to work out what to say and how to say it so that anyone can understand you.

There are a few important things to remember when thinking about professional communication. The first is that words are not enough; presentation, timing, images and design are now just as important in attracting and holding the audience.

Second, think about where these skills are leading you: that is, if you are a student, about the kinds of jobs that might be available to you with these skills. If you are already a professional communicator, you need constantly to work on improving these skills to reach changing audiences and to match more sophisticated technology. Or, if you work in another capacity but undertake some communication duties, to learn how to go about meeting demands for professionally prepared communication material.

Even if you do not want to enter any of these fields directly, this book provides you with a basic understanding of the concepts behind preparing, writing and presenting information, which you can apply to a whole range of professions.

Today, communicating is an essential skill for almost every job. Just take a browse through the weekend papers and employment sections and note how many jobs call for communication skills. The emphasis is on both verbal and written communication skills, and this book gives you a basic grounding in some of the more popular forms now used.

1

How to write effectively

How many times have you read something that you simply cannot understand? Sometimes, no matter how often you read a piece of information, its true meaning is still unclear. Good writing ensures that people understand what you are trying to say the first time they read it. The quality of written communication, and its presentation, have an enormous impact on the way in which readers absorb and react to information. Good written communication is about knowing what it is you are trying to communicate. Clarity and simplicity are vital, and obscurity does not work. Each piece of communication and every event you organise should be well planned to meet a specific aim and objective. It should also clearly and concisely convey your central message.

The basic rules for professional writing are to keep your messages and words simple, ensuring that your meaning is clear. Good writing is not just about fancy images or embossed papers; these merely add to the presentation of your message. If you remember these two basic rules and combine them with an understanding of your audience, your writing will be on the right track.

WHAT IS YOUR AIM?

Your writing, whether for an advertising supplement or a brochure, will often need to reflect the ideologies of your organisation or client. Your task is to capture, clarify and reproduce the ideas of your chief executive officer, or another group of people in your organisation, in a way that can be understood and accepted by your readers. Writing sometimes involves a different set of tasks (other than reflecting your organisation's ideologies), such as persuading someone to buy something or merely providing information. It is important to find out what drives the need for the writing and to match your writing style to the overall objective of the message.

It helps to use words that appeal to the reader. The words you choose should focus on the reader, rather than on the writer: for example, 'Your business is important to us', rather than 'We want your business'. Your writing should always be clear, to the point, factual, grammatically correct, and most importantly it should anticipate and answer the reader's questions.

Professional writing usually fulfils one or more of the following functions, in government and non-government organisations:

- It provides precise and detailed information about your product, service or organisation.
- It creates an image in the reader's mind of your product, service or business.
- It makes the reader want to buy or use your product, service or business.

AUDIENCE

You should get as much information about the intended reading audience as possible. Make sure you know who they are, find out about their education level, socioeconomic status, gender, political preferences and anything else significant about them. You can do this through your marketing department.

The audience is the most important factor of any writing, so know who you are writing for and who will be reading it. As a communicator, you will often be torn between writing for your manager and writing for your audience. This can be a frustrating and difficult balancing act, but keep in mind that both of these groups can be classified as audiences. The types of writing covered in this book target a range of people, from executives to employees, shareholders, community groups, the media and specific publics. Find out who you are writing for, discover the information required by your audience, and integrate the messages you want to give them.

Generally, the formats we refer to in this book require adopting a direct style of writing. This writing style is used to gain your reader's compliance with your organisation's messages, and is useful in brochures, newsletters, promotional kits and columns. It is a less formal style of writing, and can include tactics such as addressing the audience directly by using terms such as 'you' and 'I'.

A good rule to follow when writing anything is to put yourself in the reader's shoes. Think about how you, as a member of a particular audience, would like to be addressed and what you would like to read. Find out what you or your clients want to say, not how to say it; this comes later. Write a summary of your project before you start writing; that way you will know where you are going and what you are writing. Make sure you know the topic and do your homework. Do not try to fool the reader into thinking you know about your writing topic if you do not know.

PREPARING COPY

Professional writers usually prepare copy from an informative or persuasive point of view. The former is used to provide information about a service, product or issue, while the persuasive style is aimed at making the reader act in a certain way—to buy or use your product or service. These styles can be combined as part of another strategy, such as image creation, where anything you write is part of establishing and entrenching the image of your service or product in the reader's mind.

Most organisations will have a house style guide, which you should use consistently for all publications. These style guides include details about punctuation, capitalisation, spelling and style for in-house and external publications produced by your organisation. If you do not have an in-house style guide, you can get this information from a published style guide (such as the one mentioned at the end of this chapter).

It is vital to evaluate your writing by having other people check it. You should also evaluate the success and acceptance level of the information you provide by seeking feedback from your audience.

THE KISS PRINCIPLE

'Keep it simple, stupid' or 'Keep it short and simple'

This principle has been used for years by a variety of writers, particularly journalists. The basic theory behind it is that if you keep your writing simple anyone will be able to understand it. This is a fine principle to follow in professional writing because you can never be sure who is reading your writing, and applying the KISS principle will ensure that it is accessible to readers. There are some who suggest that you should write to the level of your audience, but keeping it simple means that your messages will not be misunderstood. The following sentence does not use the KISS principle: 'It is fruitless to become lachrymose over precipitately departed lacteal fluid'. When the KISS principle is applied, this becomes: 'It's no use crying over spilt milk' (Seitel 1995). Remember, when using KISS it is important not to treat your readers like idiots: no-one likes being talked down to.

WORDS WITH POWER

When you are preparing the kinds of writing we talk about in this book, you should pay attention to and consider the power of certain words. Powerful words are useful in persuasive writing—where you want to persuade people to your point of view or towards a particular kind of action. These kinds of words can also arouse your readers' emotions or help them conjure up certain images. It is always a good idea to get other people to read your writing and then to ask them what kind of effect it had. Martin Luther King's famous speech with its particular phrase 'I have a dream' is a good example of powerful writing.

WORDS THAT HURT

Writing has developed a lot in the past few decades, and certain descriptions and words are no longer appropriate. For example, language that stereotypes people because of their race, religion, gender, physical appearance or mental status is no longer acceptable. Words and images are able to shape the way the reader perceives and then treats certain groups. You can check with government offices—say, departments that deal with immigration or disability services—about whether they have publications that provide guidelines in these areas. The other option is to refer to a published style guide.

COLLOQUIALISMS AND SLANG

You should avoid colloquialisms and slang in your writing. Colloquialisms involve sayings or words that are peculiar to one geographical area or group of people, while slang is an informal, non-standard way of speaking. Avoid colloquialisms because your readers will often be from areas or groups that do not use such sayings or words, which can lead to misunderstandings. Slang is generally not used, as it can be considered impolite and can offend or be misunderstood.

Using active voice

The opposite to active voice is passive voice. The kinds of writing styles we refer to in this book are best produced using active voice. Passive voice makes sentences sound boring, while active voice brings a certain element of liveliness to writing. In active voice the doer of the action is the most important element, and you should always try to put the 'doer' at the start of the sentence. For example, the following sentence is passive: 'Not much is being done to offset health benefit costs by the employer'. You can make it active by rewriting it as follows: 'The employer is not doing much to offset health benefit costs'. In professional writing it is important that your writing does not sound too formal. Passive voice tends to make sentences sound formal and awkward, while active voice will help your writing take on a friendlier tone.

WORDS + IMAGES = DESIGN

Although this book is about writing, the way you present your words has a major impact on the way the reader perceives and understands them. If you have no experience in layout and design, the best advice is to get help. Do not try to desktop-publish your brochure or newsletter just because your organisation has a new computer program. Most printing firms have graphic designers who are competent in layout and design. They can do the work for you and provide a more professional end-product. Public relations companies also provide desktop-publishing services, but unless your organisation already has a contract with a PR firm you should try your printer or an independent business.

Recently there has been an explosion in small desktop-publishing businesses. Find a few, ask for prices, and get samples of their previous work so that you know they have the skills that your communication tool requires. Below are some suggestions for designing the kinds of writing pieces we discuss in this book.

Design solutions and ideas often come before you have actually written anything. Sometimes you will have a great idea for a design but you have not yet written the information or developed a plan for your writing. Write your first draft and think about design later. This way, there is more chance that the design will suit your words, and you can avoid having a wonderful design that has nothing to do with the content of your writing.

You should be familiar with the purpose of the message and design around it. Your message is the most important element in any communication tool. If you want to sell something, then your design needs to reflect this; if you are merely providing information, then you need to ensure that your design is reader-friendly but can contain all the necessary information.

Think of design as a process for solving communication problems. How can that wonderful design you really want to use get the message across more effectively and efficiently than another design?

Make sure that your message communicates what it is supposed to using original images. It is easy to use clip art and existing images or tried and true designs and graphics to communicate. Try alternative approaches that have not been used before, but make sure your graphics suit your messages.

Consider the problems of communicating your message and how you can solve or minimise them. Sometimes approaching the problem from a different perspective provides an innovative design idea for your communication tool.

Redefine the problem: for example, if the aim is to communicate the features and benefits of a new make and model of car in a brochure, your design might take the shape and form of the car and its features.

Your designs should work with and complement any messages you are conveying to your audience. Make sure your design does not overshadow or compete with the content of your writing. If your copy is important enough it will tell its own message: it does not always need graphics or images to make an impact. Simple, strong statements make the best impression when you are writing, and simple and strong images are most effective. If you are looking for artwork, remember to check copyright on any photos or graphics that you use. Artists can provide artwork, but costs vary greatly, so check first. The best graphics for communication tools are often based on the most common images that people identify with the message you are trying to get across.

If you are designing a layout, make sure you use white space effectively. White space is any area that does not contain copy or graphics. It is important not to trap white space in the middle of copy or groups of graphics: it is best used at the edges, top or bottom of pages, and particularly around headings.

Finally, get help. You should not try to do it yourself without the knowledge or the necessary skills.

HOW TO START WRITING, AND SOME RULES

1. Organise your writing: outline your piece and how you will approach it.
2. Outline the basic messages you want to get across: all professional writing needs to have a theme. A theme is usually an objective: for example, you might want to persuade someone to do something.
3. Be clear and exact.

4. Stick to the facts.
5. Avoid words with more than one meaning.
6. Get a thesaurus, so that you can choose simple words instead of complex ones. Pay particular attention to your words to avoid repeating specific ones.
7. Use simple sentences instead of convoluted ones.
8. Use one idea per paragraph.
9. Use one, or at most two, sentences per paragraph.
10. Maintain a logical order for sentences.
11. Avoid generalisations.
12. Be specific, provide details.
13. Avoid repetition.
14. When you are writing the copy, where possible use the present tense with words such as 'is', 'will' and 'are', allowing readers to relate to the issue as though it is happening now.
15. You should put important information at the start of your writing, as readers may have 'switched off' by the time they get halfway through.
16. Use active rather than passive voice (see the Introduction on writing).
17. Avoid jargon, although this depends on your audience. Do not overload sentences with technical terms: remember, your audience in an organisation may be diverse, and not everyone will understand the jargon.
18. Contractions can be used if you are adopting a friendlier tone with the audience: for example, 'can't', rather than cannot; 'won't', instead of will not; and 'I'd', the contracted version of I would.
19. Draft, draft and redraft.
20. Get someone else to check your spelling and punctuation.
21. Take your time to edit and re-edit it. Give it to someone else, or several other people, to check. Test it on a focus group to ensure that the information is

easy to read and appropriate to the audience. Focus groups usually involve members of the target audience reading and discussing their reactions to your material. If your organisation has a marketing department, it will be able to organise this for you.

FURTHER READING

Kessler, Lauren and McDonald, Duncan 1996. *When Words Collide: A Media Writer's Guide to Grammar and Style.* Wadsworth Publishing, Belmont, California.

Seitel, Fraser P. 1995. *The Practice of Public Relations.* Prentice Hall, New York.

PART I

Publications

2

Brochures

Brochures are an extremely serviceable, but overused communication tool. In fact, the overuse of brochures has led to major problems with acceptance. If you want a brochure to communicate a message, or a series of messages, then extensive homework and preparation is vital or your brochure will quickly be categorised as unproductive or irrelevant.

A brochure is useful for providing detailed information about services or products, but you need to be sure that people are going to read it. Reading anything longer than a few sentences takes time, and many people avoid this. For a brochure to succeed, your audience not only has to be prepared to read it: it has to be interested in the information you are providing—interested enough to seek that information out. There is a large degree of self-motivation required to read a brochure, so you should make sure it is the appropriate way of getting your message across.

WHAT ARE BROCHURES?

Brochures come in a variety of shapes and sizes, colours, designs and styles. They generally contain detailed information about an issue, service or product. They are designed so that people can pocket them to read at their leisure. A well-written brochure will inform your target audience, and will be easily understood and remembered.

Before you start writing a brochure you need to ask yourself this simple question: do you need a brochure? Too many people use brochures as an easy solution to their communication problems, without knowing the answer to this important question. If you spend some time thinking about why a brochure is more useful than other available communication methods and considering the issues raised here, you will be well on your way to ensuring that your brochure is read.

Start by establishing a communication objective for your brochure. In other words, think about your reason for using this medium. A solid objective should include such issues as the amount and type of information you need to convey, and the audience you are targeting. Once you have thought this out, and if you decide that this is the right medium, you should establish an objective for the overall communication of messages through the brochure. You will need to consider exactly what information is to be conveyed.

The next issue to grapple with, before you start writing, is deciding what the audience needs to know about the topic. You can do this by running focus groups or by talking to the market research department of your organisation about the most commonly asked questions on that issue. (For example, if you were preparing a brochure as part of a wider immunisation campaign, you might select parents as members of a focus group and ask them what information they most needed about immunisation.) It is crucial to include what the readers want to know, so that they will be interested in the material. If you are writing a persuasive brochure you will need to combine this reader-oriented approach with the information that your organisation wants to communicate.

How to start

Before you start writing, ask yourself the following questions:

- Why a brochure—why not an advertisement, poster or media release? What is it about the project that requires a brochure?
- Who are you targeting with your brochure? Make sure a brochure is the appropriate communication tool. For example, there is not much point in writing a brochure for a group of people with literacy problems. Research is vital to get information about your readers, such as their reading skill, socioeconomic and education levels.
- What is the objective of the brochure? What messages do you need to get across to the audience and how much information is involved? Is the information detailed or are there just a few key messages?
- What does the audience want to know about the issue and what do you need to communicate to it? How do these two things fit together? Can you make the commu-nication tool perform both of these jobs?
- Do you have a budget for your project? How much money can you spend on researching the audience and on producing the brochure?

Once you have answered these questions you can start working on some other details:

- Identify the size of brochure needed for your project and whether the size is adequate for your information needs. Check whether it needs to fit into a brochure stand and which size is best for this. Will the brochure fit into a standard-sized envelope if it is going to be distributed by mail?

- How many colours are you going to use? A two-colour brochure is cheaper to print, but full colour looks more effective.

WRITING BROCHURES

Copy for brochures should be simple and limited. Apply the KISS principle (see the Introduction) so that you do not make the mistake of trying to fit too much information into your brochure. The information age has led to a demand for facts in short, bite-sized pieces. By constantly referring to the objective you have developed for your brochure, you should be able to provide relevant information.

Start your brochure by listing, in point form, the major messages or pieces of information you want to tell your readers and then turn these points into headings. Elaborate on the topics covered in the headings with short, punchy sentences.

The writing style you adopt for your brochure depends on the kind of strategy you are using to convey the information. These strategies are similar to those outlined in Chapter 3.

Strategies

Informative

Provision of information on an issue or service: for example, a brochure that lists sexually transmitted diseases and details of where to find and how to contact your nearest sexual health clinic. The writing style adopted for this is often reasonably formal, but it depends on your audience. If your brochure is aimed at a young audience, a friendlier, less formal tone is best.

Persuasive

Information written in a way that is aimed at persuading someone to buy your product or accepting your point of view. For example, a brochure about a new stereo or car will detail all the reasons why you should buy this product. Persuasive strategies usually adopt an assertive tone and such words as 'you', which makes the reader feel that the brochure was specifically written for them and that it is directly addressing them.

Entertaining

Few brochures use this strategy on its own. It is a great idea to combine an entertaining approach with a serious subject, as long as you are targeting the right audience. For example, if you are writing a brochure on a serious issue such as sexually transmitted diseases, some light humour might help readers feel more comfortable and relaxed with what can be a serious and difficult subject.

CHECKLIST FOR WRITING BROCHURES

Chapter 1 contains many useful hints about writing that you can apply to brochures. However, below are some suggestions that apply specifically to brochures:

☐ Use simple, attention-grabbing headlines for the front panel of your brochure, with other smaller headlines to point to information inside the brochure. Headlines are easier to read when they are not printed over graphics. Avoid questions in headlines: the job of a brochure is to provide answers for its readers. Feature the main points in your headlines and expand on them in the body copy. Make sure your headline points to the specific information contained below it.

☐ Divide the main facts into areas or headings and list these in order of their importance to readers. Follow this format in your brochure, with the most important information at the start and other facts in descending order of priority.

☐ Transmit your enthusiasm for the subject to the copy, but do not exaggerate. For example, one organisation that was having considerable difficulties in attracting staff to a remote area decided to produce a brochure detailing the benefits of the area. In the brochure there were several mentions of the great beaches and opportunities for recreation in the area. Those great beaches were actually three hours from the town and the recreation opportunities consisted of a pub and an overgrown football field.

☐ Include details about topics where necessary, but avoid including trivial information that will overload your brochure or blow it out to an unmanageable size. Make sure you include contact numbers and addresses.

☐ Unlike the writing style some communicators adopt for newsletters and other writing formats, you do not need to quote an authority within the copy of your brochure. However, make sure you include your organisation's name, logo, and contact details such as address and phone number. The back panel is a good place for such details. This provides the readers with the feeling that the information is authentic and lends an air of authority to the publication. Do not include names of employees unless you intend to reprint the brochure regularly. Including names can cause problems for the public, particularly if the staff mentioned leave your organisation.

BROCHURE DESIGN

The kind of design you adopt for your brochure should be relevant to the audience, but you will need to consider the amount of information you need to convey. Brochures can be A4 size, printed on both sides and folded in a variety of ways, such as in half, or twice, where you end up with three panels of information. Some communicators use odd sizes such as two sheets of A4 paper joined together and folded several times, which produces an accordion-type effect.

Some brochures are full A4 size and contain several pages, while others are an A4-sized page folded in half, which is called A5. There are many size options and it is best to talk to a professional printer about these. Remember, paper sizes vary in different countries, so always check the names and sizes of paper with a printing firm.

You need to ensure that graphics and design elements in your brochure contribute to the messages being conveyed. For example, if you are talking about shopping in Singapore, make sure that the photos are of Singaporean shops and not of retail outlets in Hong Kong. You would be amazed at how often the wrong photos are used to illustrate brochures. Astute readers sometimes pick up these errors, and such mistakes can destroy your credibility.

Figure 2.1 is an example of a page from an A4 brochure promoting tourism in Queensland.

CHECKLIST FOR DESIGNING BROCHURES

☐ Make sure your design is simple, with distinctive artwork, using appropriate layout techniques and typefaces. Avoid the temptation to go overboard and add design elements simply because you can.

☐ Give your brochure a consistent appearance. Use linking features—for example, one typeface for all headlines and a different, but complementary, one for body copy. You can repeat certain graphics throughout your brochure to create links between the various sections.

☐ Use dominant elements such as typefaces and graph-ics on the cover of the brochure. Photos, artwork and designs should be high-quality, clear, and linked to the central message. Your target audience will avoid your publication if it has a poor cover design and substandard artwork. Invest some extra money, effort and time and hire a graphic artist to do the artwork and even the layout and design.

☐ Find out what readers want to know, select the main points, and provide a contact number for more information.

☐ You do not need to fill up every space on a brochure. Use white space: this is great for creating professional-looking documents. Use plenty of white space around headlines so they stand out and catch the reader's eye. White space can be used to focus attention on certain information within your publication.

☐ Use a reasonable-sized type—nothing below 10 point. Remember, type sizes vary according to the font you use, so make sure it is easy to read. If your brochure is for senior citizens, then 12 point will assist them to read it easily.

☐ Sketch a layout of your brochure so you can see what it is going to look like. Draw a series of lines to represent text in your brochure. Thick lines indicate headlines, and thinner lines, body copy. Try several different combinations until you decide what looks best. Once you have a good combination, replace the lines with words.

☐ Always establish rationales and objectives for your project. Keep referring to them throughout the various stages of development of your brochure. Keep them on hand in case you are asked to justify any elements of the project.

The Capricorn Coast

Forget expensive

hideaways,

out-of-the way

retreats and

unmentionable

boredom.

Just think

Capricorn Coast

The Capricorn Coast is exciting, diverse and breathtakingly beautiful. This magnificent coastline sweeps along the Pacific Ocean just 30 minutes east from Rockhampton in Central Queensland.

A scenic highway joins the main townships of Yeppoon and Emu Park, along which you can enjoy one of 13 glorious beaches. Views from the beaches and headlands are of the Keppel Islands - your stepping stones to the Great Barrier Reef.

Yeppoon is the gateway to the Capricorn Coast, featuring a charming esplanade with grassy knolls, palms and play area which form a backdrop to a vista of sea, sky and islands. The township is memorable for its seafood and variety of accommodation including Bayview Tower International. Emu Park, the home of "The Singing Ship", is also worth a visit with cafes and restaurants,

accommodation, a public pool and idyllic beaches.

Visit famous Great Keppel Island with Keppel Tourist Services on their comfortable 30 minute trip by fast catamaran, departing from Rosslyn Bay daily. Enjoy a fun-filled day on the Reef Haven Pontoon, or enjoy a visit to the Middle Island Underwater Observatory. Flights also service the island from Rockhampton Airport. Startling white beaches surround the island and bushwalking and natural flora and fauna offer interior adventures. Accommodation is available to suit any budget, from Great Keppel Island Resort, Keppel Haven, Keppel Kampout (18-35s) and a YHA youth hostel.

Moor your boat at Queensland's newest award-winning marina at Rosslyn Bay, where you can also charter a fishing boat for a day or a week. Rosslyn Bay Inn Resort and Beaches Bistro have excellent accommodation and food on offer - surrounded by lush gardens and a swimming pool.

Fifteen minutes' drive north of Yeppoon nature lovers will discover Byfield State Forest and Capricorn International Resort. This elegant but friendly resort has five-star accommodation and dining facilities, a convention centre and two international

standard golf courses. Their 22ha of wetlands are often compared in beauty and diversity of wildlife to that of Kakadu. Byfield State Forest offers cool seclusion and a rainforest environment. Dip in the lucid waters of Stoney or Waterpark Creeks, shop at Nob Creek Pottery, picnic in the recreational grounds or stay over at a log cabin at Fern's Hideaway.

Become reacquainted with nature on the Capricorn Coast, cuddle a koala or hand-feed a kangaroo at the Cooberrie Park Flora and Fauna Sanctuary. Call into the fascinating Koorana Crocodile Farm where visitors can hold a friendly crocodile and enjoy an informative tour. Stop at the Capricorn Hearts Flower and Tea Gardens and enjoy the many varieties of tropical blooms over a cup of exotic tea.

For the more adventurous, Capricorn Adventure Tours offer adrenalin pumping action - from skydiving, abseiling and rock climbing, scuba diving, paintball and horse riding to learning to fly a plane!

Whether you island hop, enjoy good food, adventure or companionship, Capricorn Coast has it all. Visit now and be prepared for a truly memorable experience filled with Islands, Beaches, Rainforest and Reef.

Figure 2.1   A page from an A4 brochure promoting tourism in Queensland

GETTING HELP

Brochure writing and design can be a daunting prospect for the new communication professional. It is a good idea to get some help the first few times you produce a brochure before having a go at it yourself. While printing firms will be able to provide help with designs through their in-house graphic artists, they will not always have staff who specialise in writing. So if you want help with writing the brochure you will need to approach a public relations firm, a freelance editor or a desktop-publishing firm. If you approach the last for help, make sure they have someone who has written brochures; you can even ask to see some of their work before you sign up as one of their clients. Some public relations companies can provide everything you need, from writing through to designing and printing, but you pay considerably for their expertise. Sometimes it is cheaper to get help from the other sources mentioned here.

Shop around, check out the costs involved with each step, such as writing, designing and printing. Another good idea is to go to an organisation that has plenty of brochures, such as a tourist information centre, and see what brochures stand out. Think about why they stand out and try to incorporate those features in your brochure.

PREPRINT CHECKLIST

☐ Has someone else checked spelling and punctuation?
☐ Do you have all necessary artwork?
☐ Do you have a written quote from the printer covering all details?
☐ Have you decided how many and what colours you are going to use? Have you seen the colours in the Pantone Colour System? Have you thought about the effect the colours have on the readability of the material? Do the colours complement each other, or do they establish effective contrasts?

☐ What kind of paper will your brochure be printed on? Does it reflect and add to the overall impression you are striving to create? For example, recycled paper creates the impression of a caring organisation, while high-gloss paper gives an expensive appearance to your project.

☐ Are you supplying the brochure to the printer in printed form or on disc? If it is in printed form and you are using more than one colour, are you supplying separate artwork for each colour? If you are supplying it on disc, does the printer have compatible technology? Have you done a test run to make sure your disc is compatible with their system?

☐ How many copies are you printing? Most of the cost for printing is in the set-up, so check how much difference there is between 5000 and 10 000 copies. Sometimes it pays to get extra copies printed to save future expense.

☐ Do your photos or artwork have to be scanned into a computer program by the printer? You may be able to save some money by doing this yourself as long as you have the right equipment and knowledge.

☐ Does the printer have a job card for your project, listing your requirements and contact number?

☐ Make sure that only one person liaises with the printer, as terrible confusion can arise when more than one person is involved.

☐ Have you discussed and agreed on a delivery date for your project with the printer?

☐ If the brochures are to be folded in a particular way, have you stipulated this and included this work in the quote?

☐ Do you want the brochures in bundles of 50 or more for easy distribution? You will need to explain this to the printer.

3

Newsletters

Newsletters have become a primary source of communication in many organisations. They have become very specialised, because they can be written, designed and distributed to specific markets, making them a popular communication tool. Today, the newsletter provides a channel for communicating with employees at all levels, also with a variety of external audiences such as shareholders, donors, volunteers, service-users, residents and customers.

The convenience and accessibility of desktop publishing has had a major effect on newsletters. Organisations and individuals are now able to produce professional newsletters more easily and cheaply than the more traditional forms of publishing allowed.

Good writing and design are important to a successful newsletter, but an effective distribution system is vital. Good writing and design are useless unless you know who you are writing for, and how you are going to get the newsletter to that audience. Once you have a basic understanding of writing and designing them, variations on the main elements of your newsletters will improve readability and access.

This chapter deals primarily with newsletters for internal audiences; it briefly covers newsletters for external audiences, but much of the information on internal newsletters can successfully be applied to external ones.

WHAT IS A NEWSLETTER?

The purpose of any newsletter is to tell its readers what they need to know. Finding out what they need to know is as important as knowing who you are writing for, which determines the style you will adopt for your newsletter. There are several different approaches you can take to your newsletter, including producing it as a straight information conduit, using it as a means of persuasion or as entertainment. Some newsletters use more than one of these approaches (see also Chapter 2).

Informative

With this approach, you are presuming that the audience is already interested enough to read your newsletter. The informative approach is used for newsletters that are part of public campaigns, for example the latest medical campaign designed to increase immunisation uptake, or the electricity industry and its recent consumer education campaign on electricity and safety in the household. Internal newsletters also take this approach, providing information about new policies, or new standards and procedures.

Persuasive

This kind of newsletter is written in a way that attempts to bring someone over to a certain point of view or attitude, or to persuade them on some issue. It is used by organisations trying to increase their market share. For example, some finance companies send out newsletters in an effort to attract new clients or to retain existing ones. This approach also targets consumers who have not yet made up their mind on a particular issue.

Entertaining

Most newsletters use entertainment as a secondary method of getting information across to the reader. All newsletters should be designed to tell readers something, and entertaining them while they read, while difficult, can be a very successful approach.

Other strategies that newsletter writers use include combining any of these tactics with emotional strategies or an image creation or strengthening strategy, designed to imprint the product or organisation on the reader's mind.

External newsletters

You can use any combination of the above approaches to external newsletters, but the most important thing to keep in mind when writing is the audience. These newsletters usually have a much broader readership than internal ones and so the kind of articles you include, particularly the mix of articles, will be different. For example, you probably would not include the bits of social news that are regularly contained in internal newsletters, such as which employee had a baby or a birthday recently.

The types of article you include will depend on the type of organisation you work for and your newsletter's audience. Most articles in an external newsletter will involve trying to persuade your audience to certain actions—such as buying, using or trying a product or service—or it will provide information on issues (for example, information for animal-handlers on the dangers of animal-borne diseases).

Articles for these newsletters can come from internal sources, particularly in-house experts in whatever field you are focusing on, or you might seek articles from experts outside your organisation. For example, a political newsletter by the local member of parliament would contain articles about what he or she has been doing lately, as well as some words of wisdom from higher sources, like the Prime Minister or a high-profile politician. Obviously the stories in this kind of newsletter would be political, but they could range from a profile of a long-standing member to a postmortem of the last election on a local, state or federal level. The other source of copy, particularly for the persuasive newsletter, is your readership. Testimonials, which are stories outlining the advantages of a product or service from a reader's perspective, can be used effectively to persuade other members of your audience of the benefits of buying your product.

External newsletters usually have a larger circulation than internal ones, and you will have to establish distribution networks and update mailing lists regularly to ensure that they reach their destination. This will involve either posting the newsletter or including it as an insert in another publication, such as the local newspaper. Check the cost of posting compared with other distribution methods (e.g. hand delivery). Your distribution method will depend on the number of copies you want to send out and the geographical area to which you want to circulate the newsletter.

NEWSLETTER SIZES

Newsletters come in various sizes and shapes, and it is vital to ensure that the format and length you choose for your newsletter suits the readers' needs. It is not sensible to produce a tabloid-sized newsletter of 24 pages if your readers have limited time and you find yourself struggling to fill it each week or month. When thinking about these issues you need to consider yourself as well as the reader. Distribution methods can also affect the size and length of newsletters. For example, if you are distributing the newsletter through the mail, small formats will save on postage.

Most newsletters are either A4 size stapled together or tabloid size, which is about the size of an A3 page. When you print an A4 newsletter it is printed on both sides of an A3 page turned sideways, which means that if you need to add pages you usually need to go up in increments of four pages. You can add one, double-sided A4 page to your A4-sized newsletter, but it will have to be a loose-leaf insert as it cannot be stapled in. Some newsletters are larger and fold out, but these are best avoided because they are difficult to handle and suit a limited audience. Sizes vary in different countries, so talk to a printer to find out specific paper sizes, their names, and their size in millimetres or inches, so you know the exact page dimensions.

You can publish weekly, fortnightly, monthly or quarterly, according to the purpose of the newsletter as well as your readers' needs. If you need to get information to your audience regularly, you will have to ensure that it is published on time and reasonably often, say weekly or monthly. This will build up some expectation in readers, and they will start to look for the newsletter at around the same time each week or month. If you are publishing weekly you may need to consider using a shorter format than you might choose for a monthly publication. The more often you publish, the faster the information in each newsletter dates.

AUDIENCE

Before you start writing your newsletter, it is important to get as much information as possible about the people who will be reading it. You will need to define your newsletter according to its purpose—particularly, what information you want to give readers and what information they need and want. It is here that finding out about your readers' educational, economic and cultural backgrounds, and their interests, will ensure that the newsletter is read and not ignored.

Thousands of organisations throughout Australia and overseas publish newsletters, but only a small percentage would know exactly why they use a newsletter rather than another communication tool to convey information. Developing an aim and rationale for your newsletter and constantly referring to these can keep you on track and ensure that you are using the right medium for your messages.

Newsletter writers are often faced with a wide range of readers within an organisation. For newsletters servicing diverse audiences, the best approach is to pitch the newsletter at a mass audience, making sure that it has general appeal and is written at a level that everyone can access.

If your newsletter is for a very specific group of people with shared interests, your writing style and presentation can be more directed, focused and reflective of the people you are targeting. If your newsletter is made up of staff contributions and is aimed at staff, it should be protected from groups such as management. Often management will try to insert information such as management directives into a successful staff newsletter, but this tactic will only put readers off.

Everything you write should be clear, logical and easily understood, so avoid clichés and jargon. A good rule is to write to the reading level of a 14-year-old, which is what many newspapers use as an audience reading level base, but do not simplify your style to the point that the information becomes diluted or superficial.

PLANNING

Planning is vital to the success of any newsletter. Set some objectives for the newsletter and your communication with readers, and always assess its success and appropriateness as you proceed.

If you are considering establishing a newsletter, ask yourself the following questions:

1. Is it a newsletter that you need, and why?
2. Whom do you want to read it and how can you get them to read it?
3. What is the purpose of the newsletter?

Once you have answered these questions you will be ready to start the following steps:

1. Choose a format, size and length and frequency.
2. Decide on the quality of your newsletter and how much money you want to spend.
3. Prepare a budget for production.
4. Develop a strategy for your messages.
5. Select your content.
6. Establish a set design.
7. Choose a name/title.
8. Develop an editorial policy and design guidelines.

The time you invest in planning will be well spent and well rewarded. If you follow these guidelines your newsletter will be consistent in style and content.

The next group of tasks includes:

- collecting information
- writing the stories
- editing the stories
- writing the headlines
- getting photos/graphics
- copy-fitting (i.e. laying copy and artwork into your design)
- editing (including checking for errors; get someone else to do this)
- liaising with printers
- distributing the newsletter
- evaluating its effectiveness and impact.

CONTENT

You need to walk a fine line between what you want to tell readers in the newsletter and what they want to read. Continually getting feedback from readers will help you to achieve this. Seek feedback by personally contacting readers. Feedback sections in newsletters generally have low success levels. For internal newsletters some researchers suggest a mix of 50 per cent information about the organisation; 20 per cent of employee information, such as on likely benefits; 20 per cent about the company's competitors or what the organisation is doing within the community; and the remaining 10 per cent of personal information and banter (Bivins 1992). External newsletters usually have a more direct purpose, and each article will have an objective. Avoid chatty information in these newsletters, as your readers will not always have enough time or desire to read these kinds of stories.

Some of the things you need to think about when planning the content of your newsletter include:

- Are you going to have columns—that is, regular articles, usually by the same person or department, covering particular themes or issues?
- Are you going to include a table of contents? This appears either inside the front page or as pointers on the front of the newsletter. A table of contents is a list of the articles inside the newsletter.
- Will you include regular announcements, such as internal vacancies, promotions or new staff?
- Are you going to have a letters column? This can be valuable for receiving feedback about your newsletter or particular issues.
- Will there be an editorial and who will write it—the organisation's chief executive officer or the newsletter editor?
- Will there be a calendar of events of interest to readers?

TOPICS

There are numerous topics that you can cover in a newsletter. Here are some ideas:

- future plans for the organisation
- personnel policies and information
- productivity improvement
- job-related information (e.g. new processes, policies or procedures)
- the financial or competitive status of the organisation
- news from various departments

- the organisation's stand on issues
- community involvement
- personnel changes and promotions
- financial information
- stories about employees
- personal news ('hatches, matches and dispatches').

Most employees are looking for information about what is happening in their organisation. You should make contact with people at all levels and keep in touch with them regularly.

Newsletters are best written in journalistic style to give them the authority and weight that is carried by newspapers, and readers will already be familiar with this style. Good news writing is also tight, easy to understand, and provides a consistent style. Keep articles brief, as many people have short attention spans or simply do not have the time to read reams of information.

FINDING STORIES

You get story ideas from a range of sources, including management, employees and departments. Receptionists, personal assistants, gardeners, cleaners and janitors are often great sources of information. You will also need to decide whether to include photos in your newsletter and, if so, whether these will be contributed by staff or taken by a professional photographer.

Find stories that will interest your readers, not just stories that management wants to see in the newsletter. Sometimes you will have to use all your skills to 'doctor' a story that management is pushing, in order to make it interesting to readers.

There are two main approaches to generating newsletter copy: you can get staff members to write articles for you, or you can interview the staff involved in the issues you need to cover and write the articles yourself. The first option sounds the best, but gives rise to a variety of problems. Although it is your responsibility as the editor of your newsletter to make copy readable, you will find some staff who will not appreciate your clean, clear copy and who might try to bureaucratise it. Stand your ground; do not be swayed by staff who want to turn your 15-word sentence into one that contains 80 words.

If you choose to write the articles yourself, you will need to interview people who know about the topic to get detailed background information from them. Although you may not use the background information, it will help in avoiding errors or having to contact the source about minor details. It even helps to get the contributors to check the accuracy of your copy when you finish it, but make sure they are aware of the ground rules about changing articles. A good ground rule is that changes to factually incorrect information will be made, but changes to the writing style are not allowed. You need to reinforce the fact that, while they are professionals in their field, you are the professional writer.

For more hints on news writing see Chapter 9, on media releases. With each article you write you need to have some idea of what it is that you are trying to achieve. For example, if you are writing an article about superannuation, it may be that company employees have been grumbling about the money garnished from their pay for this and that you need to explain the benefits of it. Writing a brief objective for each article will ensure that it is relevant to readers.

LEADS

A good lead sentence is essential in order to capture and hold the reader's attention. If you are writing straight news, then lead with the news, as that is the most important piece of information in the article. Your lead needs to present the most important piece of information about the issue, and you can follow it up with details in order of their importance to, and connection with, the lead.

Include direct quotes for effect, but do not overuse them and take care not to repeat the information in them in other parts of your story.

When editing submitted articles and even those you have written, look for useless information and repetitions that can be cut without changing the quality and content of the story. A third edit should indicate where sentences can be tightened.

HEADLINES/CAPTIONS

Headlines should sum up the content of the story in a few words, but avoid using too many small words like 'in', 'on', 'at' and 'the'. Use short words that portray the precise meaning of the story, so that readers will quickly be able to identify stories that pertain to or interest them.

Captions should sum up the content of a photo. Avoid stating the obvious in the caption, such as:

Heather Brown holds a sand bucket while working on a sandcastle at the beach yesterday.

It is not necessary to explain to readers what they can already see in a photograph. Instead, tell them what events led to the photo, for example:

Budding architect Heather Jones has a long way to go before her sandcastles become real cities, but if her mini sand city construction is anything to go by, she is off to a flying start. Heather was one of many children enjoying the fine weather at the beach yesterday as part of the city council's fun day.

SOME OTHER HINTS

It is important to ensure that your newsletter is consistent, and one of the methods for doing this is to follow up on stories. It is useless having a story in the April edition about a new product being developed, or new staff who have been employed and then forgetting to say anything about the new product when it is ready to launch or the new staff when they arrive. Also, if you find yourself with space to fill, do not just go for articles from the nearest brochure or a similar newsletter because these are covered by copyright; it will be obvious to readers that this was a last-minute thought.

PREPRINT CHECKLIST

☐ Have you checked dates, spelling, punctuation, grammar and accuracy?

☐ Do you have the right issue number on the newsletter?

☐ Do you know how many copies you need printed?

☐ Have you obtained a written quote from the printer covering all costs?

☐ Do you have all the artwork, photos, graphics, colour separations?

☐ Do you have a distribution system and mailing list in place?

☐ What kind and colour of paper are you using? If it is recycled, make sure you write that on your newsletter.

☐ What colour ink are you using? Some colours, particularly yellow, should not be used.

☐ Have you settled on a completion date by which the newsletter must be printed?

☐ Will the printer deliver the newsletter to your office, or do you have to collect it?

☐ Do you have an official order form or another method of payment (account numbers etc.) established with your office and the printer?

☐ Does the printer have a quality-assurance program?

☐ Have you booked your newsletter in to the printer for printing?

☐ Do the printers want hard copies of your newsletter or can they accept it on a disc? If they can accept a disc, make sure the printer has the same computer program and the same kind of system. A good idea is to take a copy of your newsletter to the printer, on disc, in advance to see that their computer system really can read it. Check that your formatting, such as indents and type sizes and fonts, is the same on the printer's computer system.

PRINTING NEWSLETTERS: GETTING HELP

Check whether your organisation already has a relationship with a printer. There may be a special contract between your company and a local printer, which may involve discounts for certain jobs.

If your organisation does not have a printer, the *Yellow Pages* will usually provide a starting point to identify printing firms. Choose three and fax them a detailed outline of your job. In this case you would send a fax listing details such as:

- number of pages
- type of paper required
- number of colours used (two colours is much cheaper than full colour)
- number of photos or other graphics
- time frame for the printing of the newsletter
- what kind of binding (also called stitching by printers) you require (for example, do you want stapling and if so how many and where will the staples be inserted?)
- whether or not you want it collated
- number of copies
- whether any desktop-publishing assistance is needed

- whether colour or black-and-white photos
- whether you need to supply bromides of logos or scanned images.

Most printing firms have graphic designers who have experience with a variety of desktop-publishing applications. They can assist you with design if you have difficulties. Printing firms are usually more than happy to explain their requirements for producing newsletters, and will even take you through the printing process so that you have a full understanding of their needs.

Another option is to approach a public relations company for assistance with any aspect of your newsletter. Public relations companies can advise on what kind of newsletter to print, and may even be able to undertake some market research on your behalf. They can produce an entire newsletter, including collecting information, writing stories, designing and printing, or they can undertake any of these services individually. Freelance editors or desktop publishers can also provide some or all of these services. Of course, these services will incur additional production costs, so you may like to enrol in a desktop-publishing course and then do it yourself.

FURTHER READING

Ranly, Don 1991. *Publication Editing with Exercises: For Editors of Consumer, Trade, Corporation, Association, Public Relations, Public Information, and Organization Publications of All.* Iowa State University Press, Ames, IA.

Bivins, Thomas 1992. *Fundamentals of Successful Newsletters: Everything You Need to Write, Design, and Publish More Effective Newsletters.* NTC Business Books, Lincolnwood, IL.

Avieson, John 1993. *Desktop Publishing a Newspaper.* Deakin University, Geelong, VIC.

Blatner, David 1991. *Desktop Publisher's Survival Kit.* Peachpit Press, Berkeley, CA.

Webb, Eric and Lovelock, Marjorie 1990. *Looking Good: Desktop Publishing.* Australian Government Publishing Service, Canberra.

4

Reports

Most reports are boring, too long, costly, and most importantly are not read. As a professional communicator, you will often be called on to prepare these documents, from committee reports to your organisation's annual report. Preparing reports that are readable will be a test of your skills as a professional communicator.

Reports can be a valuable communication tool—especially something as significant as an annual report. However, many organisations make the mistake of filling reports with boring information whose only achievement is to send the reader to sleep.

What you should strive to achieve in any kind of report is a fluent writing style that communicates the right amount of information about your topic, in an interesting way.

WHAT IS A REPORT?

Reports can range from a short account of your activities and achievements over a week or a month, to much longer, more researched and detailed work, such as an annual report. Reports come in a variety of formats, including:

- short reports, which can be covered in letters or memos;
- issue reports, detailing the latest information on particular issues;
- informative reports, such as those which detail progress on a case;
- regular reports (e.g. monthly activity and cost reports);
- justification reports, to explain why you want that money for a new computer or why your department needs a Porsche to drive clients around the city;
- statistical reports, providing information about the number of people using your services etc.;
- annual reports.

Most reports are in a written, narrative format. If this is the style you choose, you will need to present information in a clear and logical order. You will be responsible for choosing the layout and headings for it. The other style adopted for reports is a preset format, where headings and layout are already established and you write information in the spaces provided. Preset formats are often used for financial reports.

Whichever method you choose for your report, it will usually be either analytical or informative in style. Analytical reports analyse information, presenting solutions to problems and giving the reader an overview of the issues associated with the report topic. An analytical report could focus on the problem of too many committees in an organisation. The report would investigate the existing committees and their activities, while providing an analysis of why there are so many committees and why they are failing to achieve anything. It would also outline one or more solutions to the problem. Information-based reports provide details, but not analysis. This kind of report could provide details of what you have achieved during the past month, but it would not provide any analysis of those achievements.

AUDIENCE

When you are writing a report you need to consider the person or people who will be reading it. The language you use and the way you write it (for example, whether you adopt a casual approach or a more formal style) will depend on who is going to read it. If you were writing a report for your organisation's chief executive officer, you would probably use a formal tone; if you were writing a report for your supervisor about your monthly achievements, you might be slightly less formal. Make sure you find out who will be reading the document before you prepare it.

WRITING REPORTS

Reports should contain an introduction, body and conclusion. The amount of information contained in each of these areas varies according to the content and type of report. In an analytical report the introduction outlines what the report is about, the body contains the information you are discussing, and the conclusion summarises and presents recommendations for actions. A report that is merely presenting information can also use the introduction, body and conclusion format, but it generally will not contain recommendations.

How to start

- Find out what your report is about.
- Work out what information you need to present, think about the areas the information falls into and create headings for these.
- Write the headings down, and sketch in details of the information required under each heading.
- Make sure the most important headings are at the start of the report. Once you know who is going to read your report, you will be able to determine the order of your headings. It is important to order your headings so that

readers are easily able to find the information most relevant to them.

- Choose a title. Your title should tell the reader what the report is about and contain all the major details of the report. It is not enough merely to call a document an annual report: you need to include the name of the organisation presenting the information, the year the report pertains to, and the area covered by the organisation. It is vital to indicate whether reports are drafts or proposals or are the final document.

STRUCTURING REPORTS

There is a variety of approaches used to structuring reports. Once you have a basic structure from which to work, you will be able to adapt it to suit your purposes. The following is a basic format that people adopt for reports.

Introduction

This, the first section of your report, should provide an outline of what the report is about and, if it is analytical, its major findings and recommendations. Your introduction is where you have a chance to impress the reader with your clarity and conciseness, so use this opportunity. It should establish your reader's expectations about the information that follows.

You should outline who you are, so readers know who is writing the report, and your experience or qualifications in the area the report covers.

Provide some information about who initially requested the report. Discuss the origins of the report and why a report was required. Make sure you tell the reader what the report is about in the introduction, so that they can decide immediately whether it is relevant to them.

The introduction should outline the report's goals and objectives. This information will also help the reader understand what he or she is reading. A report's introduction gives a brief overview of the information to be presented in the body of the document. You should indicate how you obtained the information in the report; for example, did you interview or survey employees? As the report writer you need to identify other people who were involved with the preparation of the material and list their credentials.

A good way of setting out your introduction is to create headings and allocate each heading a number. For example, you might label your introduction as follows:

1. Introduction. You would then label each of the sub-headings under the introduction:
1.1 Terms of reference
1.2 Objectives
1.3 Methodology.

Your introduction should include all the major facts and discuss the results of your investigation as well as hint at the major recommendations you make elsewhere in the report.

Keep the introduction as short as possible. Make each subheading a short section that helps readers to find information quickly. Your readers should be able to follow your line of thinking about why you approached the issue the way you did, and understand how and why you came to your recommendations.

Body

The next section of your report is commonly referred to as the body. This is where you present the results or the main information you have collected. You should divide this into sections that relate to the main areas of information you are covering. Create some headings under which you can group pieces of information.

You would identify this section of the report as follows:

2. Body. Subheadings within this area could appear as:
2.1 Interviews with staff
2.2 Interviews with management
2.3 Interviews with owners
2.4 Interviews with government.

The next section, still in the body of your report, would need to discuss the results of your interviews. You could call this section something like analysis or discussion:

3.   Discussion. Subheadings would be labelled as:
3.1 Need for change
3.2 Advantages and disadvantages of change
3.3 Costs associated with change
3.4 Other issues.

Include diagrams, tables, pictures, graphs and other supporting documents or information that will help to get your message across.

A third section in the body of your report would outline the recommendations you are making to resolve the issue. You would call this:

4.   Recommendations. Present each recommendation as a single point.

You might label these recommendation 1.1, recommendation 1.2 and so forth. Do not try to put too much information in the one point. Separate the issues you are talking about and make as many recommendations as you need to cover everything. Your recommendations should be logical and related to each other, as well as to the central issue of your report. Provide specific information in each recommendation, such as how your organisation might go about implementing it. Be forceful: for example, if something has to be done, say it has to be done. If you think some recommendations will not be accepted, include alternative options. If the issue needs more investigation, say so.

Summary

The final section of your report, apart from any appendixes such as questionnaires or articles that you want to include, should be the summary. This should merely reiterate the main points and findings of your report. Make sure you sign and

date your report and include your contact details, your
position title, and the organisation's name.

PRESENTING REPORTS

1. Start with a solid idea of what the final report is going
   to be about.
2. Decide what kind of information you will be using
   in the report and why you need to include it.
3. Use opinions, but make sure they are easily read as
   opinions and not confused with facts.
4. Make sure people want to read, understand and be
   persuaded by the report.
5. Set the report out clearly, using simple, concise language and explaining terms.
6. Use the same format throughout (e.g. the same num-
   bering system).
7. Headings and subheadings will break the report into
   easily absorbed components.
8. Avoid long passages of text; 'bullets' are great and
   can be used to break up large areas of text.
9. Provide summaries of information in all sections.
10. Use tabs, particularly within sections, to differentiate
    between main points and subpoints.
11. Illustrations of any kind are fine, but they must relate
    to the information you present and add to its readability.
12. Use white space, especially around headings.
13. Make it easy for the reader to find information by
    using readable fonts, with larger and bold type for
    headings.

WRITING ANNUAL REPORTS

One kind of report that professional communicators are
constantly asked to prepare is the annual report. Your
organisation may have special requirements for its annual

report, so always check. It is a good idea to gather past copies and look through them to identify the type of information required (see Figure 4.1). Some companies have to meet governmental statutory requirements in their annual report, so find out whether yours does and if so obtain an exact list of these. Your annual report should be used as an effective communication tool as well as meeting the organisation's legal obligations. Many organisations pay a lot of money to produce annual reports, so make sure you get your money's worth by making it perform for you.

Most annual reports will have a section that contains budget information. You should not prepare this information unless you are an accountant. Work with your finance officer and discuss requirements for setting out the information. He or she should provide it to you in a ready-to-print format.

Your organisation may impose restrictions on hiring outside agencies to assist you in preparing your annual report. Find out what the rules are and follow them. Annual reports are a big undertaking for a single person, so if you are able to hire outside help to collect and prepare information, it might pay you to do so. Public relations firms, desktop-publishing organisations and even freelance editors can be called on to help with this task. You will need to direct the operation and ensure that written quotes are obtained, while providing a guiding hand for the production of the report.

The contents of your annual report will vary according to the type of organisation you work for. However, you should include basic background information about the organisation; a chief executive officer's or chairperson's report; reports from major departments or sections of your organisation; a list of the major achievements of the year; and financial information. You should also keep in mind that graphics and photos can assist in conveying information to the reader, so these should not be overlooked. Most annual reports are A4 size, and the number of colours and the quality of paper you choose will depend on the image that you are trying to convey.

The year ahead will provide us all with exceptional opportunities to build upon the advancements we have made in 1995 in the key areas of Safety, our conditions of employment, the performance of the Business, and the Expansion Project.

Our Safety Performance is improving with the Implementation of the SafeWork Programme and our goal will be to ensure a much higher percentage of the plant meets the required Safety Standards. We gained a great deal of value from the Incident Investigations in the past and the actioning of the recommendations will yield a safer workplace.

I am enthusiastic about the opportunities offered to employees and the Business alike, from the introduction of staff conditions of employment at our other Smelter Sites. At BSL we have made tremendous progress towards this goal and I will continue to take the necessary steps towards providing you with this choice. The statewide support has been overwhelming and we will arrange for more employees to experience work secondments at our other Smelters to assess for themselves the distinct benefits of staff conditions of employment.

The technical performance of the plant is showing signs of improvement from the significant efforts made last year. It has been an important step forward as we prepare for the expansion of the site. All areas of the site will be touched in some way by the expansion. We are seeing already the arrival of new employees, construction is well advanced and development opportunities for individuals have been well received. The expansion is delivering a new technology which will enhance the overall performance of the business, but most of all it is delivering us a chance to develop. There has been, and will be more training and skills acquisitions for employees at all levels in the business. A sizeable portion of this work will be overseas to enable key people in the expanded plant to successfully operate the new technology.

We have a challenging and exciting year ahead and I invite all employees to share in it.

General Manager's Report

Adele Brown
Lynn Lapham

Brian Bassett
General Manager

Figure 4.1   A page from an annual report

PREPRINT CHECKLIST

☐ Have you met legal and government requirements?

☐ Has someone else proofread it for you?

☐ How many copies do you need?

☐ Does it reflect your organisation's image?

☐ Have the financial reports been approved and signed off by your audit office?

☐ Have you followed any guidelines that restrict the type of report you can prepare?

☐ Have you decided how many and what colours you are going to use? Have you seen the colours in the Pantone Colour System? Have you thought about the effect the colours have on the readability of the material? Do the colours complement each other or do they establish effective contrasts? (Do not use bold colours if your organisation is conservative.)

☐ What kind of paper will you use for the report?

☐ Do you have a written quote from the printer covering all details?

☐ Have you stipulated how you want the report stapled or bound, in the spine or in a corner?

☐ Do you have a signed and dated agreement with the printer?

☐ Have you settled on a delivery date with the printer?

☐ Are you going to provide the annual report to the printer on disc or as hard copy?

☐ Is the printer's equipment compatible with the computer you have produced your initial report on, and have you provided a sample disc to ensure this?

☐ Have you provided instructions about the printing of graphics and photos?

☐ Have you given all graphics, photos and other information to the printer?

FURTHER READING

Sedgwick, D. Glenn 1985. *Annual Reports: The Annual Expense*. School of Management, Deakin University, Melbourne.

Brock, Susan L. 1988. *Writing Business Proposals and Reports: Strategies for Success*. Crisp Publications, Los Altos, CA.

Cheung, Anthony C.M. 1996. *Writing Business Reports: Student's Book*. Intercom Press, Sydney.

PART II

Promotional material

5

Advertisements

What is an advertisement, and what are its functions? If your organisation wants to hire new staff, or let people know about an upcoming event, or communicate a position to a wide audience, you will need to advertise.

An advertisement is space that is paid for in order to carry specific messages. There are two main types of corporate advertisements, which can be understood in terms of two different purposes or functions. The first type is classifieds, which has such functions as:

- attracting staff
- public announcements
- tenders
- public notices.

The main purposes of classifieds are to provide information and to get a response. Classifieds should not have a persuasive or rhetorical aspect: the idea is to attract an audience to the ad, and to enable that audience to provide your institution with the information it needs to proceed with the task at hand. (For instance, once you know the person's qualifications and experience, you can decide whether to short-list him or her for a position, whether to call for referees' reports, whether to readvertise.)

The second type is 'displays', which are used for:

- attracting staff
- promotions
- advocacy
- attracting a field to a vacant position
- improving consumer relations
- presenting an institutional position on a public issue
- improving the image of the institution
- countering criticism or bad publicity
- improving employee relations.

Classifieds are normally located at the back of a newspaper, just before the sports section, although in some newspapers there are detachable classified sections. Classifieds are normally single-column, although display classifieds can be two to three columns wide—and considerably more expensive.

Whereas classifieds deal with information, displays can be about information or perceptions, depending on the subtype of advertisement. They often make use of persuasive or rhetorical language if their purpose is not so much to get a specific response from individuals as to change the way people view the institution.

One important thing to take into account, if you have a choice between classifieds and displays, is cost. Classifieds are less expensive, and seem less prominent, but at the same time readers will automatically go to the classifieds to look for advertisements. Compare the various rates you will be charged (for columns and lines), and balance this against the point that classifieds have consistent and wide readerships.

WHAT IS A CORPORATE ADVERTISEMENT?

What general principles characterise such advertisements?

First, the advertisement should convey an image that represents and reflects the values of the organisation. Corporate advertisements always have a practical function (we deal with these different functions later in this chapter). But as well as having the more specific function of, say, advertising for staff or announcing a corporate function, advertisements are one of the more obvious ways in which an organisation 'communicates itself' to the public.

Advertisements end up in the public domain, and they are accessible to people that an institution might normally not deal with or see as part of its immediate audience. Just because an advertisment is directed at a specific market— people in a particular profession, or company shareholders— does not mean that the larger public will not see and read it, and subsequently judge or evaluate the institution in terms of the image it presents in the ad.

These days most institutions have recognised that advertisements have a twin purpose: there is the specific, matter-at-hand function; and there is the opportunity for wider public exposure. Every time an institution advertises itself, it has the opportunity of raising its general recognition level.

The communication of an institutional image will, to a large extent, be carried by the visual and layout aspects of an advertisement. At the same time, content can be crucial: if an institution is trying to project an image of itself as caring and customer-focused, then an advertisement which ignores or contradicts this image is not doing its job—regardless of how effective it is in terms of its more specific function. Before preparing an advertisement, care should be taken to ensure that the message—whatever it is—is informed by an appropriate corporate image.

Second, the effectiveness of an advertisement will depend on the extent to which there is a match between content, layout, timing and placement on the one hand, and purpose on the other. This requires planning and research on your part. You will, of course, have a considerable say in the content of your advertisement: you will be expected to provide content which is clear and thorough but minimalist.

Making decisions about content comes down to having a precise understanding of what is to be achieved by the ad. Your institution does not merely want a staff counsellor: they might want five years' experience, tertiary education qualifications, and a willingness to work weekends in out-of-town locations. These are distinctive and significant features that potential respondents need to be alerted to—otherwise you could be wasting your institution's time and theirs. You do not have to include every possible detail—only that which will give your target audience the information it needs (e.g. who, what, when, where, why and how).

You will probably not be doing layout for the ad, but you should know what the institutional style is, and be prepared to make suggestions to graphic artists or personnel about any variations or modification to that style that will serve your purpose. For instance, if you are producing a job advertisement, you will probably want something that attracts the widest possible readership, which perhaps means making prominent use of corporate logo, headline and white space to help the ad stand apart from other job advertisements. If the main purpose of your ad is to supply information—say to shareholders, who are expecting an ad about an upcoming meeting and primarily want to know when and where—layout will be less of an issue.

The important point is that you should be clear as to the kind of graphics and layout you require, and check that you have been given what you needed.

Timing and placement are not always given the same emphasis as content and layout, but they are often just as important. Planning and research are the keys here. If you are given an advertisement to write, you need to find out: what time lines are involved; what is the audience; and what kinds of publications they are likely to read.

Time lines are important, if only because they tell you how long you have to write the ad. If you have only a short time to attract job-seekers, or to notify the public about an institutional function or initiative, that will have an effect on where you place the ad. The best place to attract a wide field of psychologists or counsellors might be in a professional journal, but if it comes out only once every three months and you need to appoint somebody soon, you might be better off placing your ad in an up-market, high-circulation newspaper, which will get you an immediate field.

PREPARATION

There are four main stages to preparing the advertisement:

1. Check with contact people regarding facts and dates.
2. Determine what the purpose of the ad is, and what is to be accomplished.
3. Marshal all the facts, and make decisions about editing the possible content.
4. See the graphic artist about how the ad is to be put together, and always consult about when and where it is to be placed.

   Discussions should include reference to:

- headlines
- the body of the ad
- artwork (and photographs)
- the institutional logo
- white space
- contact names and adresses, and relevant dates.

You should always check the results—and refer those results to the contact persons—before you let anything go to publication.

WRITING THE ADVERTISEMENT

The advice we have given you in other chapters about how to write applies equally well to advertisements.

With classifieds:

- Work out what ideas or information are central.
- Put those ideas, or that information, up front in your advertisement: if the purpose of your advertisement is to call for tenders for a project, start with a statement to that effect and then provide relevant details about the institution, the work, time frames and contact persons.
- The body of the advertisement should carry the detail that you are trying to communicate. This should be divided into clearly differentiated sections (such as specific qualifications, job description, institutional contexts or background) of one paragraph.
- Include any points that will tie the advertisement to your corporate image, such as references to institutional mission statements, policies, or mottos, but keep them brief, and preferably at the end of the advertisement ('The university is committed to putting students first', or something of that nature).
- Normally, an advertisement will conclude with details as to where enquiries should be directed, and application closure dates and requirements.

See Figure 5.1 for an example of a classified advertisement.

With displays:

- Identify the problem, issue or message that needs to be tackled or communicated.
- Start with a statement about the problem or issue (such as 'The university has been associated, in recent media reports, with allegedly dubious marketing practices').
- The body should then work off, and around, that initial statement, putting or refuting an argument or claim, or clarifying the institution's position.

Notice of Preparation of Board of Directors Report

Yuletide Industries Pty Ltd

Notice is given that a report about the affairs of Yuletide Industries Pty Ltd has been prepared pursuant to section 4321(z) of the Corporations Law, and has been lodged with the Corporation Commission. Any person can, on the payment of the prescribed fee, inspect this report at the Commission office.

Dated 25 December 1997
S. Claus Managing Director

Figure 5.1 An example of a classified advertisement

- Work in references to the institution's mottos, policies or image ('A caring institution').
- Conclude with something positive, such as a reiteration of the institution's commitment to certain goals, values, standards or practices.

See Figure 5.2 for an example of a display advertisement. Remember:

- to use short sentences
- to stick to one idea per paragraph
- to keep paragraphs brief—as brief as one sentence in most cases
- to use everyday language, avoiding jargon or technical language if possible
- to make sure that you have complied with institutional or industrial protocols or policy requirements (such as a

SPORT AUSTRALIA'S COMMONWEALTH SPORTS GRANTS

Government Financial Grants to Assist Local Sports Clubs

Sport Australia provides financial assistance to non-profit making sports clubs at local level for projects such as building clubhouse facilities, youth coaching schemes and organising regional competitions.

Applications are sought from clubs for any of these or other relevant projects that will commence 1 July 1998.

Phone 01 1111 6789 Fax 01 2222 3456
APPLICATIONS DUE 1 FEBRUARY 1998

Applications must use the appropriate grant application forms, which can be obtained by phoning or faxing the above numbers, or by writing to the Department of Sport, GPO Box XXX, Sydney 2000. Forms may also be downloaded from our website http://www.ds.au/grant

The Department of Sport

Figure 5.2 An example of a display advertisement

reference to an equal opportunity employment policy). Check with previous organisational advertisements to see how these things have been done in the past.

The best way to guard against problems is to consult the staff of the publication in which you are placing the advertisement, such as:

- the advertising manager
- the classifieds coordinator
- the display advertisements representative.

Give them your contact numbers, so that if anything goes wrong you can respond quickly. And make sure that you know how the publication's advertisement section works (who to contact, during which hours, how far in advance they require bookings, costs, and other similar details).

ADVERTISEMENTS FOR RADIO AND TELEVISION

In certain circumstances, such as if you want to promote an event that is coming up quite soon and you want to get the widest possible coverage, it may pay you to advertise on radio or television. Radio is good if you are running out of time (an event is on in a couple of days' time, and you want to ensure a good turnout of the public). Radio advertising can be relatively expensive, so you probably would not use it for promotional or image advertising; television might be more appropriate.

Check rates for different radio stations, as regionals can be cheaper than metropolitans. Costs will vary depending on the program, production costs and frequency of advertising.

Whom do you contact? Both radio and television stations have 'advertising and promotional managers' or perhaps 'sales representatives' that you need to deal with. It is important to shop around if you are looking to advertise on radio or television, because costs can vary considerably, particularly in peak times. If you have been quoted a lower price by one station, let their competitors know—they might be able to match or beat it.

What time slots do you use? This depends on the urgency of the event, the target audience, the medium you choose, and your budget. If you are using radio and need to reach a wide audience, anything but prime time/drive time is not going to be of much use to you—but this will be expensive. Television has a wider prime time, but the slot you choose should be determined by the target audience: talk to the television sales representative about when 'your' audience is likely to be watching.

What do you have to provide to radio or television sales representatives? They may require a script, but more likely they will simply want to know the background, the purpose and the target audience. Normally they will produce a script and visuals, which they will get you to check and respond to. You might be required to be there for any filming that gets done at the organisation—to show a camera crew around, or to make arrangements with staff so that shooting can take place.

CHECKLIST FOR DISCUSSIONS ABOUT RADIO OR TELEVISION ADVERTISING

You need to know:

- ☐ the names and numbers of station sales representatives
- ☐ the rates they charge for different lengths and time slots
- ☐ when they can fit you in.

They need to know:

- ☐ the background, purpose and target audience
- ☐ contact names and numbers of relevant people in your organisation
- ☐ when they can film at your organisation (if it's television).

FURTHER READING

Wilcox, D. et al. 1992. *Public Relations: Strategies and Tactics.* HarperCollins, New York.

6

Advertising supplements

An advertising supplement or advertising feature generally comprises four main elements:

- stories
- advertisements
- graphics and
- photographs,

and is a supplement to or additional feature in a newspaper. An advertising feature can vary in size from one page to 64 pages or more. The beauty of this package is that other businesses that want to advertise and promote their involvement with your venture will also be contributing to the cost of the feature.

The best reason for producing an advertising supplement or feature is to boost your advertising campaign with others helping to foot the bill. Advertising supplements or advertising features are a valid and efficient way of conveying 'sales' and 'news' information to newspaper readers. Whether you are opening a new restaurant or promoting a service, the combined effect of stories, graphics and advertisements will generally far outweigh any of these as individual elements.

Usually an advertising feature is used when there is not enough space—in a press release, a photograph or an advertisement—to convey your message, and to ensure you get what you want in print. Because putting a feature or supplement together requires a lot of work and organisation, you should decide whether you really need the whole package. You may feel a news release or photograph will do the trick, but it is unlikely that the editor will include 'marketing' or 'advertising' information such as prices, product information, phone numbers and addresses. There is also no guarantee that your press release or photograph will be used, or, if it is, that it will appear where and when you would like. Perhaps an advertisement is what you require. This will run when you want, where you want, and with the 'sales' content you want. The problem here is (as mentioned in Chapter 9), that people tend to believe information that has been 'screened' by the editor—the news—before anything else in the newspaper, such as advertisements.

BENEFITS

One benefit of an advertising supplement or feature is that you can combine the credibility of 'news' stories and photographs with the 'straight sales' information of advertisements. Another benefit is that by putting together a supplement or feature on a particular topic you can get other interested advertisers to contribute to the cost of the space. For instance, you are starting a new restaurant and you decide to put a large feature in the local newspaper to let everyone know you are opening soon. Other people involved with the restaurant, such as the builders, outfitters and suppliers, will be keen to promote their contribution to the new venture. They may want a small story in return for their advertising support, but the more businesses involved, the larger the feature and the more attention it should bring your business.

DRAWBACKS

One of the major drawbacks to doing an advertising feature or supplement is that it does not have the credibility of a straight news story, as it is generally identified at the top of each page as an advertising feature or advertising supplement. In other words, readers know you have paid for the space, so still have reservations about the content. This can be overcome to a certain degree by taking particular care with writing and producing the supplement. The other major problem is that putting together an advertising supplement, even if only one (newspaper) page, can involve a lot of hard work, particularly the coordination of editorial copy and advertisements. Nearly every newspaper will have people working in these roles, but the more you are involved, the closer the final product will be to your expectations.

PRODUCING A SUPPLEMENT

Producing a newspaper feature or supplement is much more than simply writing a couple of stories on your product, service or organisation. You should consider seven major aspects:

1. advertisements
2. size/circulation
3. colour
4. editorial
5. photographs
6. graphics/layout and
7. production.

As originator of the feature you take on the role of editor and advertising manager—not one to be envied. The best advice is to set firm deadlines for all contributors at least a week ahead of your own deadlines.

Advertisements

The newspaper's advertising department or advertising features department (if there is one) is your first port of call. Many regional, and most metropolitan, newspapers have a features department, which includes journalists, editors, photographers, advertising representatives and often a graphic artist and features coordinator. You will start with the features coordinator, who will then allocate an advertising representative to work with you. The advertising representative or advertising consultant who is organising your feature should be looking after your advertisements. However, you need to be able to guide him or her as to the content of your ads, and then coordinate and supply copy, photographs and graphics. You also need to provide a list of potential additional advertisers, including contacts and phone numbers. Make sure you talk to the businesses first, though. Builders, suppliers, outfitters and even the bank or financiers of the project may be interested. If you are in a centre or complex, neighbouring businesses may also want to support your efforts to bring more people in.

Do not try to cram a huge assortment of facts, figures, photographs and graphics into your space. That is why you chose to do an advertising supplement in the first place—to give yourself space and the variety of elements to get your message across. Some of the most memorable advertisements have consisted of just one line on a whole page. Use your advertising space—probably half a page—for your main points, prices, phone numbers, address and other 'sales' and contact details that do not fit well in your 'news' stories.

You have the added advantage that within this space you are free to use artwork and a variety of graphics and typefaces that would look out of place in your editorial space. This is also the place for the persuasive 'sales' words (specials, bargains etc.) that do not suit your editorial. The number of pages in your feature will to a certain extent be determined by the number of advertisements. Most newspapers have a set rate of editorial and advertising percentages for their pages, and this also applies to advertising features and supplements.

Size/circulation

The best way to look at an advertising supplement is to consider that you are producing a mini-newspaper. The size could range from one page to 64 pages or more, depending on your needs and budget, and those of the other participating advertisers. The ideal is to have at least four pages, the centre pages, so it can be inserted in the newspaper after printing and then retained easily by readers. If it is only one or two pages, it is printed as part of the paper (or 'run of paper') and not easily kept and, more crucially, often not easily identified or noticed as it could fall anywhere in the newspaper. For this very reason, and because inserting a 'supplement to the newspaper' requires more labour, a 'run of paper' feature is much cheaper. If you do publish your feature as 'run of paper' try to start on a right-hand page (an odd-numbered page), as these are generally more well read than left-hand pages.

You also need to decide which newspaper will give maximum benefit for your money. Ask for the demographics of the paper's readers to see if they match your target market(s). Also ask for circulation figures and areas. You may decide that a state or national paper better suits your needs than a regional—or a combination of the local newspaper with either state or national editions.

Decide what day is going to be best for your feature. In this case your new 'bush tucker' restaurant—Bush Fare—is opening on a Saturday, so the day before probably would be ideal. You may also want to print additional copies of the feature, which you can circulate yourself. You might get additional mileage for the advertising feature on your restaurant by supplying copies to the local tourism promotion centre, airport, or even by distributing copies at special expos, such as food and wine festivals.

Colour

If you decide to print your supplement separately (preprint) and insert it in a newspaper, you have the choice of either full or spot colour. This cannot be so easily guaranteed if you go 'run of paper'. Full colour is, of course, wonderful if you can afford it, particularly if you have some good photographs and graphics. However, the costs lie not only in printing but in the initial production of the photographs, and in getting colour separations of the photographs (a photograph divided into primary colour negatives for printing). If you are taking the photographs yourself, do not forget to include the cost of film and developing in your budget. If you have decided you can afford to go with full colour, and this includes photographs, it may be worth the expense of hiring a professional photographer to take your pictures for the feature.

If you choose to go with spot colour (black plus a second colour in spots of your choice), make good use of the colour in key areas you want to highlight. For instance, the headline of the main story on the page, and a box around the photograph and caption, would be ideal. Most newspapers will generally advise you to avoid yellow as a spot colour. Depending on the reliability of the press, the quality of paper and ink and the sheer strength of the colour, yellow has been known to do a virtual disappearing act when it comes to the final product. Cyan (blue) and magenta (red) are far more striking and reliable.

The rule when it comes to using colour—whether full or spot—is not to overdo it. Less is definitely more when it comes to colour. Tasteful additions rather than a riot of colour will make these touches far more noticeable and attention-grabbing.

Editorial

It may take more time, but making your editorial newsworthy and interesting will enhance reader interest and thus benefit your business. There are many definitions of what makes 'news' or a newsworthy story, but it is basically anything that people are interested in, and anything that makes people talk. People are generally interested in reading about other people, so keep this in mind when deciding on stories for your feature (refer to Chapter 9).

Because your pages have already been identified as an advertising feature or supplement, a good way to inspire credibility is to avoid any 'sales pitches' or any information that should be in ads. For instance, in your advertising feature on the bush tucker restaurant you are opening, the lead story should not be a reprint of your menu and wine list with prices. While this may be interesting for some readers, if you really want this sort of detail it should be in your ad, not your editorial. Your main story should be your biggest news story—such as the fact that the Australian bush tucker man, Les Hiddens, will be opening your new and unusual restaurant and demonstrating his culinary skills.

People are invariably interested in other people, so ensure that the bulk of your stories include the human element. There are five major steps to organising your editorial:

1. Make a list of stories, including ones that may be contributed by other businesses.
2. Choose your main story. In this case the new restaurant being opened by Les Hiddens is a winner. It combines a number of news elements—an unusual, new restaurant being opened by a prominent personality.
3. List the people who should be the focus of stories in order. Do not be shy! If you are the brains behind the operation, you should be one of the first stories.
4. List stories that might better be illustrated by a photograph and caption.
5. Arrange the list in order of importance and match them to a page. Be careful of clashes. Do not cram too many words onto a page; remember that you have photographs and graphics to add interest to your stories.

Photographs

Photographs are an important part of any newspaper, and are often described as the window to the page. Do not fall into the trap of trying to cram so much copy onto your pages that the photographs are no bigger than postage stamps. This makes the pages look cluttered and difficult to read, and generally puts people off.

Unless you are a good photographer, get a professional in. If the photographs are even slightly out of focus, lacking in contrast, colour or boring, newsprint will always accentuate the problem. The newspaper will undoubtedly have 'preferred' photographers that they deal with, and some have their own staff photographers specifically working on advertising features. You need to supply them with a list of photographs for your feature and some general ideas about what you envisage.

When you are putting together a list of stories for your feature, decide which need illustrating and how best the photographs might 'tell' the story. Most people agree that a picture tells a thousand words, and it is perhaps worth considering using a photograph *instead* of a story in certain cases. The blocklines or extended caption (words describing the photograph) will enable you to put in any identifying details you may require. When you are doing a draft or dummy layout, make sure your photos do not 'run off the page'. In other words, if you have a photograph of a car that is moving from right to left, put that photograph on a right-hand page, or on the far right of a left-hand page. This way readers' eyes are drawn into the page by the photograph, not out of and off the page.

There are five steps to organising your photographs:

1. Get your list of stories and decide which need illustrating. Do not forget those contributed by other businesses. If you are going with a full-colour feature, limit the number of colour photographs unless you have a big budget and

a graphic artist who can place them all tastefully and to best advantage.

2. Start with the main story. In this case a photograph of Les Hiddens would seem essential. The newspaper probably has publicity shots of him on file.

3. You will also want photographs of your restaurant, inside and out. The exterior shot is particularly important, so that potential diners can readily identify your new business.

4. Match photographs to your 'people' stories. Arrange interesting settings, not just straight 'mug' shots. For instance, the main supplier for your restaurant could be photographed collecting ingredients in the bush.

5. Match the list of photographs with the stories and pages. Place them for maximum benefit, to draw readers into the page.

Graphics/layout

Graphics and layout are very much like photographs: unless you have experience in this area, get the professionals to do it. However, you must provide them with ideas, examples and even dummy layouts to give them a concept of what you want. If the newspaper has its own features graphic artist, she or he will do up a 'dummy' or a 'prop' to give you an idea of what your feature could look like. If you decide you are going to do the feature, also enlist the graphic artist's help with the look of the final product. Aim for a 'clean' look, with some unfilled white space (area unused on the page), which is less cluttered and less intimidating to readers.

Typefaces

Have a limit on the number of different typefaces you use, even in your ads. Otherwise they will all be competing with each other for attention, and the pages will look too busy to read. Most newspapers use only one or two different typefaces for headlines (sometimes just one and then a bold version of that for contrast), and a complementary one for body copy. There are many reasons for this, including ease of reading.

A typeface such as 𝕺𝖑𝖉 𝕰𝖓𝖌𝖑𝖎𝖘𝖍 𝕿𝖊𝖝𝖙 would be appropriate if you were opening an Olde English Inn, rather than a restaurant specialising in bush fare.

Production/deadlines

Find out at the very beginning the sort of lead time (time required before printing) the newspaper requires for your advertising feature. Most newspapers like to see completed camera-ready (ready-to-print) pages one week before publication. When the pages are completed ask if you can view them to do your own proofreading. Your advertising contact will generally organise copies of finished advertisements to be faxed to you. Not all newspapers allow the checking of editorial, so you need to establish this at the very start.

If you are able to proof the final product, check readability (the stories should flow) and spelling (particularly names of people and businesses). Check that captions fit the photograph and that headlines are correct. Particularly ensure that details such as dates, times, phone numbers and addresses are correct. Get a couple of other people to read it as well: the more eyes that see it, the better. Most newspapers operate with full pagination these days, which means they work on the whole page on their computer screen. This eliminates the cutting and pasting of pieces prior to printing, and should reduce mistakes such as having columns in the wrong place or misplaced headlines.

GETTING HELP

There are three different ways to do an advertising feature:

1. Hire a public relations firm with the combined expertise to produce the whole feature.
2. Put it all in the hands of the newspaper.
3. Work closely with the newspaper, with you as 'editor'.

The third approach is recommended, to ensure that you get what you want. You will still have to devote a certain amount of time to briefing if you choose option one or two, and the former is quite expensive. However, if you do not have the time but you do have the budget, the first option is for you. Option two relies on the time the newspaper staff have available, and invariably they are doing a number of features at one time, so you will not always get priority treatment. Though you will be doing a lot of work if you choose the third option, ensure that, for specialised work such as the photographs and the layout, you call in the experts. Those elements produced professionally will give your supplement or feature the polish that will attract readers.

ADVERTISING FEATURE CHECKLIST

☐ Set a date *at least* one month before you want your feature published, to start the ball rolling.

☐ Contact the newspaper's features coordinator or advertising consultant to discuss size, deadlines, quantity and cost.

☐ The newspaper should provide you with a 'dummy' or 'prop' of what your feature may look like. If all is well and the price is right, book your feature in.

☐ Get a list of advertisers together. Contact them first before giving the list to the ad rep.

☐ Write a list of stories; match them to pages.

☐ Match photographs to the editorial. Organise photographic opportunities.

☐ Give other contributors a firm deadline of at least one week before your own deadline. Remember, the feature should be finished one week before publication.

☐ Give the graphic artist your draft pages, including allocation of editorial and photos. If the paper allows, ensure that the finished product is sent to you as soon as possible.

☐ Proofread, proofread, proofread. Get others to proofread.

FURTHER READING

Hunt, T. and Grunig, J.E. 1994. *Public Relations Techniques.* Harcourt Brace College Publishers, Fort Worth, TX.

Wilcox, D.L., Ault, P.H. and Agee, W.K. 1992. *Public Relations: Strategies and Tactics,* HarperCollins, New York.

7

Columns

Many larger organisations have started to use columns as a method of communication. While these columns have traditionally appeared in newspapers, some organisations have recently started to establish 'columns' or 'spots' on the radio or on television. This chapter focuses mainly on newspaper-style columns, but radio and television 'columns' are covered briefly.

WHY USE NEWSPAPER COLUMNS?

Newspaper columns come in two main styles: paid advertising or free editorial. Columns can be used to disseminate your organisation's point of view and opinions on issues, or they can simply provide information.

The persuasive column is useful for an organisation heavily involved in issues and crisis management, as a vehicle to reaffirm that organisation's stand on particular issues or involvement in certain events. For example, a column for a health organisation that appears in a newspaper on a fortnightly basis might originally be intended as an information conduit, but when services are being criticised you could make it an integral part of a media campaign to emphasise your point of view. Such a column would be useful in supplying the public with details that journalists are unable to cover in their newspaper articles. So in this case the column would become a multifunctional one. During the quieter times, when there are no issues or crises, you could continue to use it as a mechanism to update the public on subjects such as skin cancer or to provide information on special clinics and services.

Using the column for these two very different purposes may suit your needs, but a word of warning: if you start your column as an informative one and it gets taken over by the authority voices in your organisation, you may lose readers. If your column is the free editorial type, then you should avoid sales pitches and ensure that it is informative.

Whichever method you choose, it has to suit your objective. As with newsletters, brochures and a whole host of other written communication methods mentioned in this book, you need to set an objective for the communication (see Chapter 1). Once you do this, it is a simple matter of sticking to what you have set. You should also regularly review the performance of your written communication tools to ensure that they are meeting these objectives.

ESTABLISHING A COLUMN

When, how and where you establish a column will depend on your resources, objectives for communicating, and budget. Television and radio regular guest spots in metropolitan areas and even in some regional areas could cost you a lot of money. If you are working in a regional area, the range of media outlets may be fewer, but this might mean you have better access. For example, a radio session in a regional area could operate as part of a specific program.

It is not always possible to gain free access to a radio or television station, so you will need to negotiate and assess each situation. Queensland Health, for example, established an information session on a regional Australian Broadcasting Corporation (ABC) radio station in 1994. It was a 5- to 10-minute weekly session that aired as part of a regular radio show, and topics covered a wide range of health matters. As well as receiving great feedback from the audience, the staff found it an ideal mechanism for promoting health issues and services.

The initial idea for the radio session came from Queensland Health's desire to circulate more health information to the community. At around the same time the health organisation established a shopfront, which provided health information and advice to the public. It also had a column running in the local daily newspaper, but this format did not cater for those who did not get the paper or people without good literacy levels. Of course, these two audiences needed health information as much as, if not more than, regular readers of the newspaper. The search began for a way to solve the communication problem. While thinking about the problem, staff remembered that some of their rural health workers had mentioned that many of their clients listened to ABC radio. From several, seemingly unrelated issues, a solution to the problem was born.

Once Queensland Health had settled on a radio session, the next step was to contact the radio station with a detailed outline of the idea. The proposal included some objectives the organisation wanted to achieve with the sessions, a six-month plan that outlined what issues would be covered in each session, the names and phone numbers of the 'experts' who would be able to speak on each topic, and some ideas staff had about the format of the sessions. Fortunately, ABC radio was extremely supportive of the idea and, after some fine tuning, a regular health information guest spot was established. Another option here would have been to approach the local community radio station. Community radio stations are always looking for program presenters and guest speakers.

The same Queensland Health group tried to develop a similar concept for television, but this was much more trying and was eventually shelved due to a lack of funds and support. While the idea for a regular television session that provided health information from bona-fide health workers was applauded, the amount of money required to produce and air the session was beyond the organisation's means.

This concept could be successful as part of a larger commercial organisation's communication strategy. A successful television column was established by the Queensland Police through a commercial television station. The sessions provided a variety of information on topics from safety for women to speeding fines. Ford Australia has tried a similar idea, running extended commercials regularly that are presented as news reports.

PLANNING

Regular guest spots on radio and television involve a lot of planning and effort. It is a good idea to start out with something a bit easier to manage, like a regular column in your daily or weekly newspaper. If you want to try an editorialised column, the best idea is to establish a proposal including objectives for communication, some indication of the benefit to the newspaper, and a list of the topics you will cover. You will need to indicate how often and when it will appear, whether there will be one writer or guest writers for the column each week or fortnight, as well as how you would supply it to the paper—on disc or as hard copy.

Prepare a sample column. It pays to work these issues out well in advance and consolidate your ideas about the column before you approach the newspaper. This will lend your organisation an air of professionalism and give a good first impression. Contact the chief of staff and suggest a meeting (lunch is always a good incentive) to discuss the idea. Provide copies of your proposal and organise a time and date to follow up the issue. Remember, the paper might have some ideas about what the column will look like, so you will have to negotiate this. Be prepared to give some ground, because your organisation and public will still benefit from having the information printed.

Once you have established a column, it is important that you see that copy is delivered at the same time each week. You will miss out on a great opportunity to promote your organisation or issue if you do not provide the copy, and it could create the impression that you are unreliable. Plan ahead, so that you know well in advance what issues you are covering in the column.

WRITING

> It is sometimes a waste of time sitting down to write a column. A host of disconnected thoughts rip through the tiny mind and the component you most avidly seek, coherence, is the very thing which is missing . . . Anyway it is often a waste of time trying to write a column. A column needs a thread, a vehicle on which to hang various thoughts. It cannot be a haphazard jumble of incoherence . . .

Errol Simper (1996) may have been talking about the kind of column he writes for *The Australian* every week, but his words are equally applicable to the types of column we are talking about here.

A few words of warning before you leap into the column fray. Do not be fooled by eager colleagues into thinking that writing a column will be easy. As soon as you are stuck for copy, those eager beavers who sang the praises of newspaper columns for organisational communication will be heading for the hills.

If you are going to write a column, make sure you have enough information to fill it, every week, fortnight or month, depending on how often you want it published. The same applies if you are running a radio or television session. Radio and television require more planning than newspaper columns and often involve other members of the organisation.

There are two basic approaches to writing newspaper columns. The first of these we refer to as the editorialised column, and the second is what we call the advertorialised column.

THE EDITORIALISED COLUMN

The editorialised column is a column that appears usually within the feature pages of the newspaper. As a rule, you would not pay money for this kind of column. That means you would not have control over whether it appears, how much of the information you supply is included, or the actual words that make up the column.

An editorialised column needs, as Simper suggests, a thread to hang it on. You need to have a basic idea for your column and then build up the idea with facts, figures and quotes. Whether you are writing about legal issues, health information or trekking through Sumatra, you need to keep in mind that a wide range of people from diverse educational backgrounds could read it. Keep your language simple and use short sentences. Give your column to a few different people in your organisation to read. Ask them to highlight anything they cannot understand, or whether they have suggestions about how you could explain things in simpler terms. Always provide a contact number, or numbers, at the end of your column or, if you mention a specific event, within the text of the column. Figure 7.1 is an example of an editorialised column.

If you are organising a radio or television session, you will need a different approach. Radio sessions usually involve more organisation than writing, and often involve an interview between the 'talent' and the radio announcer. You will need to brief your talent—that is, the 'experts' who are going to be interviewed. You should do this a few days before the session goes to air. Prepare a list of the main points that will

Campaign offers powerful advice

onservation
oncerns
With the
Environmental Coalition

Australian businesses and industries are major contributors to the world pollution and greenhouse gas problem.

Australian industries use more electricity than their counterparts in any other developed country.

The Australian Environment Coalition wants to do something about changing the way Australia uses power. As well as cutting down on green house gas emissions, conserving energy could save Australians millions of dollars each year.

Our new campaign, Energy Wise, was launched this week. We are targeting businesses and industries that waste power through inefficient practices and machinery, as well as general energy waste such as ineffective insulation.

We also want staff of Australian organisations to take more care about using power. Leaving lights on of a night wastes a lot of energy, when a simple flick of a switch as you leave work will conserve power and save money.

Making your work place more energy efficient is easy and doesn't have to cost a lot. We offer a free advisory service that identifies the most common areas where organisations lose or waste power and steps to fix the problem.

As we move into the 21st century, we need to start conserving the Earth's resources.

Developed countries such as Australia are major users of natural resources and every industry and business as well as members of the public must take responsibility for the wise and efficient use of energy.

Households can also take steps to use power more efficiently and cut down on electricity bills at the same time. There are many small steps you can take that won't cost you a fortune.

We are providing brochures that outline the ways of making your home more energy efficient. You can collect one from our city shop front in Halligan Shopping Centre or we will post one to you if you call us on 27 6443.

Figure 7.1 An editorialised column

be covered in the session and make sure your talent and the radio announcer have a copy of this prior to air time. If your talent has not had much experience with interview situations, it is a good idea to set up a mock interview for them.

If you are organising a television session, then as well as identifying the theme for the session and the talent who will present the information you will need to prepare a script for it, including audio (what you want the talent to say) and visual (what pictures you want to show). You can apply the rules we have listed in Chapter 11.

THE ADVERTORIALISED COLUMN

The second kind of column is the advertorialised column. This is an advertisement that is paid for by your organisation. Newspaper space is sold on a column centimetre basis, so you will need to know how much space you can afford, also how much you will need to get your message across. You might be able to negotiate a special advertising rate (cost) for your column, particularly if it is going to appear weekly or monthly. Paid-for columns are good because you create a consistency to them, that you are not able to achieve or control with editorialised columns. A good idea with a paid column is to ensure that it appears on the same page, in the same position each time it runs. This format also allows you complete control (barring misfortunes and accidents) over the column's contents, layout and design. Figure 7.2 is an example of an advertorialised column.

The drawback is that the column has all the characteristics and appearance of an advertisement, so you will need to make yours look much more professional than the advertisements in the rest of the paper. Some of the elements that can be used in these kinds of columns to make them more appealing to read include graphics, photos, headings and regular sections such as staff profiles, events or research information. A combination of narrative and information in

Halligan Health Services

Sexuality and You

Our Sexual Health Service is offering you the chance to find out about the role sexuality plays in your life. Sexual health researcher Dr Joe Oxley will discuss the many complexities of our sexual identity and how we understand sex. This free guest lecture will be held at our clinic on Thursday, 17 June from 2 pm. A free afternoon tea will be provided at the end of the hour lecture. So, if you want to find out about this challenging, but personally important issue, come along.

Eating Well

Eating is a major pastime for many of us, but do you know what you eat and, as the saying goes, are you what you eat? Australians experience one of the highest rates of obesity in the world, due to our excessively fatty diets. If you want to lose weight, but just don't seem to have the commitment needed, then we might have the answer for you. Health Lifestyles is a new program being offered by our Community Health Centre. This program will guide you through food choices and help you make healthier decisions in relation to meals. It also gives you a soft exercise program, that develops as you lose weight. This way you are only doing as much exercise as you can safely handle. If you'd like more information about the program, contact the program coordinator Julie Heart on 27 8900.

Congratulations

The new Well Women's Centre has taken out the inaugural Australian Government Health Awards for its innovative approach to providing health services. The award judges said the Centre won the competition because of its friendly atmosphere, well trained and experienced staff and the focus on relaxation and art for health. Congratulations to staff of the centre for a job well done!

Project Officer Position

Halligan Hospital needs a Project Officer to join its rapidly expanding Planning Department. Responsibilities include planning for the introduction of new services and a new hospital in the year 2000. Applicants should be experienced in capital construction projects. Appointment level will depend on experience and qualifications. For a position description phone 27 6655. Applications close on August 1.

Figure 7.2 An advertorialised column

list form will help to create focal points for those reading the column.

CHECKLIST FOR WRITING COLUMNS

Have you established the following?

☐ A rationale—Why a column?
- What will your organisation achieve with the column?
- What is its purpose or objective?
- How often and where will it appear?

☐ Audience—Whom are you targeting?
- How are you going to get the intended audience to read it?
- What benefits will the audience get from the column?
- At what level do you need to pitch the column?

☐ Language—What level of language will you use?
- Are there technical terms that need explanation or is the audience familiar with them? You may pick up readers who do not have this technical background.
- What approach will you use to the column—first person 'I' or a more reserved style? Which of these appeals to your intended readers?

☐ Topics—Who is going to set the topics?
- Will you establish a list of suggested topics or will the media outlet or your manager control these?
- What topics will you cover?
- Are the topics very specific or do they cover broader and more generalised subjects?
- Have you developed a list of topics to use in the column?
- How will you ensure continued interest in the column?

☐ Authors—Will you write it and if so do you have the expertise to do this?
- Will you collect the information from the experts and edit it?
- How will the experts cope with being edited?
- How will you justify the editing?

FURTHER READING

Simper, Errol 1996. *Weekend Australian*, 14/15 September.

8

World Wide Web page

A 'World Wide Web' homepage is the equivalent, and may combine the features, of institutional newsletters, brochures, reports, advertisements, videos, directories and handbooks. Most medium to large organisations now have a presence on the Web, and it is an increasingly important way of communicating information. Many organisations create 'local area networks' (LANs), which are closed networks on the Internet used for internal organisational communication or for communication with specific groups of customers.

It is worth noting that creating an organisation's homepage can be expensive if you use an outside provider to establish and maintain it. However, it is possible to use an experienced Web designer to create an attractive homepage and then to update material in house, taking advantage of the conversation functions of popular word processing and layout computer programs. Web design is a specialised skill, and you may not have this skill in house.

What a Web page is like depends on four points:

1. its functions
2. the size, variety and complexity of the organisation
3. the type of organisation
4. the amount of information to be communicated.

A Web page usually has four main, and closely related, functions:

- to 'advertise' the institution—to let national and international audiences (including potential market audiences and like-minded organisations and interest groups) know that the institution is there;
- to provide information about the institution—its history, contact numbers and addresses, staff, activities, policies, services, products, affiliates and plans—to clients or potential clients, or merely to its own employees;
- to act as a directory that enables persons accessing the site to get to the information they want as quickly as possible;
- to provide a source of feedback.

Some organisations have single-site pages which perform specific functions (for instance, a company might put its corporate plan on a single page without much reference to the other functions, (such as advertising and providing general information about the company). Sometimes an organisation will combine all these functions, which are to be accessed through an initial homepage that performs the twin functions of advertising the organisation and directing the user to specific pockets of information.

The size and complexity of an organisation determines the kind of page you need. An organisation that is small and reasonably homogeneous (e.g. a small business) will only be out to do a few things (advertise its existence, services and products, and provide contact names and numbers). A large and complex organisation (a multinational company, a government department, a university) will still need a Web page that advertises and directs, but the bulk of the site will be made up of a (sometimes labyrinthine) complex of different levels (based on locations, departments, functions), more or less separate organisations (a union page, a research group page) and widely varying functions (more guiding, advertising, selling, recruiting, contextualising, listing, informing, explaining, taking complaints, updating activities).

Finally, other factors, such as whether the organisation is public or private, can determine the balance between advertising and selling on the one hand and servicing and informing on the other.

WHAT IS A WEB PAGE?

A Web page is, of course, different from conventional print and visual media such as books, brochures, posters and videos. It makes use of the written and the visual, but the fact that it has to perform so many different tasks means that the extent to which one or the other predominates will vary according to the sections and functions of the page.

Web pages are supposed to encapsulate an organisation and its activities on one site; and, given that it has to inform, advertise and guide all at the same time, it is important that the page be user-friendly. Below are a few principles to keep in mind.

- Language and sentence structure. Like virtually all professional writing genres, Web pages should be characterised by simple, straightforward language and short sentences. The only departure from this is if you are collecting material from a department or section that needs to use technical language.
- Do not try to fit too much material onto your homepage, and in particular do not overdo the amount of print material. Web pages need a strong visual aspect to attract and maintain the user's attention; they do not need a mass of print material, with long, undifferentiated paragraphs and sentences. Let your visuals do their work

unencumbered by a lack of space or an overwhelming amount of print.

- Simplicity, clarity and accessibility are the keys to a successful homepage. Keep the information and instructions as simple as possible: one word or sentence should be enough to differentiate sections and to guide the reader to them.
- Make your visuals, and your titles, sentences and phrases, as catchy as possible. What is acceptable in, say, a small private company is not always acceptable in a large government institution, but that does not mean you have to provide visuals and script that are dull and boring.

CONTENT

Your Web page will normally not contain too much information, but it will need to act as a directory that lets users know what information is available, and where it can be accessed. And there is information that should only go on that page; you just need to be careful when deciding what that is, how it is to be expressed, and how much space it takes up.

It is important to give your Web page a strong visual touch. You can use either representational or abstract material: it depends on the kind of image you are trying to project, and your target audience. But make sure you leave enough space for your information. Figure 8.1 is an example of a Web page.

What information is absolutely vital?

- the name of the organisation;
- its logo, crest, motto;
- a short description (one sentence) of what it is, or does;
- some contact names, addresses and numbers (general enquiries, post box, main organisational address, fax, e-mail and Web address;
- a copyright notice for the page.

Figure 8.1 An example of a Web page

And headings relating to some, or all, of the following:

- sections
- departments
- services
- products
- activities
- market groups
- staff
- latest news
- affiliated organisation(s)
- policies
- documents
- legal notices or information (about Net use, or copyright)
- Web resources
- how to access different sections, and the technology and time required
- sponsors

- frequently asked questions
- user comments/feedback
- organisational history.

RESEARCHING, PLANNING, CONSULTING

You will probably not be responsible for much more than the homepage; the other pages, and the information they contain, will be the responsibility of the relevant staff members.

Your first job is to decide what sections or categories need to be on the homepage. For this you need to make a kind of inventory of your organisation on the one hand, and to identify the needs of your clients or readers on the other. In other words:

- What do you need to tell your audience?
- What is your audience likely to be looking for?

Do not try this on your own. You do not know everything about the organisation—what it does, or its clients' needs. The best way to come up with those categories is to consult any documents on organisational structures, services and clients, and then speak to all the relevant staff (departmental heads, marketing managers). When you think you have a list of categories, check back with those staff and get their confirmation.

Once your categories have been confirmed, you need to get the relevant information from staff. Your request should be accompanied by a series of guidelines about the amount of material required, the language, and the need for names, numbers and addresses.

When you have all the information you need, go through and do an edit. Why? Because you want to make sure that the information provided is:

- consistent
- comprehensive

- clear
- not overlapping or repetitive
- in keeping with organisational policies
- in keeping with copyright laws.

As well, you probably need to do some cross-referencing between sections.

What about graphics? You might want to provide your own visual material for the homepage, but it is probably best to ask staff to provide their own accompanying visuals. Again, if there is an imbalance between visual and printed material, or if there are problems with the layout, consult the relevant staff before making changes: you do not want to edit out vital information.

You might want to make use of someone with specialist graphics expertise. A lack of sensitivity to colour, for instance, could seriously diminish the impact of your page.

UPDATING

Any information on your homepage needs to be updated regularly. This is one of the advantages the Web has over print media such as books and brochures and visual media such as videos: books and videos continue in circulation long after they have ceased to be wholly, or even primarily, accurate; Web pages can be updated from day to day, if necessary.

The best way to ensure that the material on your Web pages is up to date is to make arrangements with relevant staff to provide you regularly with new or modified details about their services, products or operations. To keep them on the ball, you should regularly send them copies of their section on the Web, asking them to verify that the material is accurate.

Finally, if you do have a client feedback page, make use of it.

WEB PAGE CHECKLIST

☐   Decide what you want the page to do.
☐   Consult relevant staff.
☐   Create a draft and circulate it.
☐   Organise the visuals and graphics.
☐   Check contact names, phone numbers and addresses.

FURTHER READING

Lemay, L. 1995. *Teach Yourself Web Page Publishing with HTML.* SAMS Publishing, Indianapolis.

9

Media releases

Many forms of professional writing adopt similar structures and styles, but this is not the case with the media release or press release. Press releases are written specifically to release information to the media, with a structure, style and content appropriate to this function. Because the media operate on tight deadlines and need to make decisions quickly about running with stories, the media/news release should convey the essential information immediately and concisely. More attention and credibility is given to news stories than to advertising because of this screening process, and they are free. Between 70 and 80 per cent of the copy in some newspapers today is generated from stories or leads from professional communicators. However, the news release must be written and presented in specific ways if you want to take advantage of this. The content must be newsworthy, and the layout clear and uncluttered.

STRUCTURE

The best way to approach writing a news release is to realise that it is not like any other form of writing. It is definitely not creative writing, particularly in terms of content. A press release should be 'nothing but the facts'. Think of some of the writing structures you are familiar with. Reports, for instance, usually start with a short introduction, have the bulk of the information in the body, then finish with the most important information summarised in the conclusion. This structure can best be described as the pyramid writing style, for example:

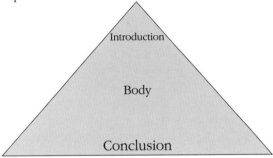

When writing a press release you have to forget this structure; in fact, you need to turn it upside down, for example:

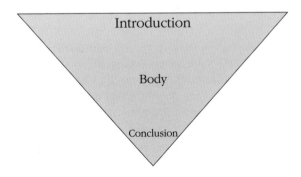

The inverted pyramid writing style was initially adopted when the media had to use telegraph wire services to convey information, a service that was unreliable and often interrupted. Journalists devised a structure to convey the most important information (news) first, in case the connection was broken.

This inverted structure places the essential information or summary at the start (the introduction), followed by other important facts (the body), with less necessary facts in order of importance (the conclusion). Historically, this meant that even if the wire connection was interrupted, the news (in the introduction) generally got through. In today's media world, where editors and news editors have to choose stories quickly—and generally only use about 3 per cent of what comes over their desks each day—this structure means that the news is not hidden and can be evaluated immediately. Also, if the story is cut back to three or four paragraphs, the 'guts' of the story is not lost.

THE 'INTRO'

This brings us to another aspect of writing a media release: paragraphs. For 'hard news' writing, one sentence usually equals one paragraph, and generally the shorter the sentence the better. This is particularly so with the first paragraph—the introduction or lead. This first 'par' must catch the attention of readers, viewers or listeners, and make them want to find out more. It must also attract journalists looking for story ideas, or for a story to use in full. If you do not catch them with the first paragraph, they will not bother reading the second. In terms of readability, or ability to take information in, the briefer the better. An introduction of about 10 words will be simple and direct enough to encourage even the busiest of readers to continue. For instance:

Flooding stopped traffic in Newcastle today.

would be more likely to encourage readers to continue than:

> The enormous amount of constant precipitation and heavy winds which was very severe and worse than locals may have seen for many years has caused havoc and stopped the flow of traffic throughout many areas of Newcastle today.

Eight words or fewer is 'readable'; more than about 25 words is getting difficult. The idea is to encourage busy readers/listeners/viewers to stay with the whole story. Considering that the average readership ability age for most daily newspapers is between 10 and 14 years, the KISS principle is essential (see Chapter 1). One rule of thumb is that in 100 words you should have no more than about 150 syllables. Writing a news release is not a vocabulary test: it is finding the way to get your message or information across to the widest possible audience. Always use the simplest words. Instead of 'commence', use 'begin', and large words like 'approximately' are practically banned in most newspapers (use 'about'). To put it simply, your introduction has to be the attention-grabber.

To ensure that you are used as a source of news by the media it is necessary to apply the ABC of journalism to anything you release. A is for accuracy, particularly when it comes to the spelling of names; B is for brevity, and the briefer you are the more likely all your information will be used; and C is for conciseness—of story, paragraphs and words.

CONTENT

Every news release should answer certain questions and supply specific information. The six essential 'serving men' (as described by journalist and writer Rudyard Kipling) are who, what, where, when, why and how. Known more commonly as the 5Ws and H, these questions should be answered in the first three to four paragraphs of your news release. Generally, if you have caught the readers' attention with the lead, they will read the next two to three paragraphs, at the very least. And if your story is cut due to space limitations, it will rarely be cut any shorter than four paragraphs. It is sometimes even worth considering keeping your news release to only four paragraphs—a good size for the 'news in brief' section of a newspaper. As any editor will tell you, this is the most well-read section of any paper.

Do not try to cram all the 5Ws and H into the introduction. Choose the most important or most newsworthy to go first. Generally it is the 'who' and the 'what' that make the news.

News

A journalist's job is to report the news first, so that is what readers will be looking for from you. What makes news? First, there is what is known as 'hard news'—information, facts, events, decisions and recommendations—as opposed to soft news, which appeals to the emotions. There are many elements that can make a story newsworthy, but the general rule is that news must have an impact on people. It must be of interest; news is about people (often widely known or prominent). To quote an old adage, 'Dog bites man' is not news, but 'Man bites dog' would probably make the front page, because it combines people and (we hope) the unusual. This theory can actually be disproved to a certain extent using the prominent-people element: if 'Dog bites man', and that man is Prince Charles, this too will make page 1.

News is often about conflict, as well as people, whether about two neighbours involved in a disagreement or two countries at war. Proximity is also important when considering whether a story is newsworthy. It is highly likely that more people in a community would read about the dispute between the people down the road than about a war between two distant countries. Currency, too, could be the angle or 'hook' you need. Is your story on a current issue that people are talking about, such as the environment, AIDS or equity? Your news release might be about an event, an unusual or exceptional situation, a scandal, breakthrough or disaster, all newsworthy. Perhaps the simplest definition of hard news is 'something that is going to happen, something that is happening, or something that has happened'.

Whichever news angle or element you choose, there is one thing your story must be—*new*. If you have what you consider to be a good news story, do not save it up!

The 'angle'

The length of the story is usually determined by the number of people affected by or interested in it. If the editor decides that a large group of people will be interested, not only will the story be longer but it is likely to be in a more prominent position. This may be on page 3 or even page 1, known as the early general news pages and most widely read and sought by journalists and advertisers. Apply the 'who cares principle' to determine how many people would be interested in a particular story. If you are the only one interested in the story, go back to the drawing board. Sometimes it is as simple as coming up with a new angle for your story, and rewriting to reflect this. For instance:

> The International Society of Investment and Accounting will be holding a full-day business accounting seminar covering areas such as annuities, stocks and futures at the Town Hall this Saturday.

is unlikely to attract anyone except the most dedicated of accountants. However:

> Find out how to make your first million at the Town Hall this Saturday.

will probably appeal to a far wider audience, and pass the 'who cares' test easily. The angle or 'hook' you choose will also depend on what you are hoping to achieve with your press release. Is it pure information, is it for publicity or promotion, or to defend your organisation? Is it as simple as trying to get 'bums on seats', as with the example above? You must decide this before you start writing.

Ensure that your story sounds *new*, even in the way you present it. The easiest way to do this is to use active voice, particularly in your lead. For instance:

At Parliament House today the Prime Minister was bitten by a dog.

does not have half the impact of:

A dog bit the Prime Minister at Parliament House today.

The words 'was' and 'by' should set alarm bells off immediately. Rewrite the story in active voice and present tense. Also, while the first example contains the news, it is 'hidden'. The where and when are not the news, but the who and what are (as is commonly the case). So check not only that you have put the most important information in your lead but also that it is not hidden. If you are still having trouble writing your introduction, put your notes away and imagine you are leaning over the fence telling the story to a neighbour, or talking to a friend or your mother on the phone. Vocalise it and start with: 'Did you hear . . .', and the rest should follow: ' . . . a dog bit the Prime Minister today . . .'.

Another hint is that most introductions are little more than extended headlines: in other words, subject, verb and object. So if you can think of a headline for your story, start perhaps with that and convert it into your first sentence.

The body of your story should follow similar lines to your introduction; it should continue in order of importance in keeping with the inverted pyramid writing style, and should also pass the ABC test of being accurate, brief and concise. Before you tackle your press release, remember that it should contain the facts, and nothing but the facts. Even adjectives and adverbs should be avoided unless they can be attributed. For instance:

> More than 2995 very happy people attended the wonderful school fete last Saturday.

should be:

> About 3000 people attended the school fete last Saturday.

Unless you have gone around and confirmed that everyone is very happy, this is not fact, and if someone thought the fete was wonderful, you should have them saying it. When attributing statements to someone, avoid using the term spokesperson with no name: the media give more credence to statements where the source is identified. Editorial comment is for the editor, and comment or opinion can be expressed through letters to the editor. If your media release is more a reminder of an upcoming event, you might just send the essential information bullet-pointed for emphasis. For further style hints, analyse the media to which you intend to send your press release.

PRESENTATION

Remember, news releases are not only written in a certain way for the media, but are presented specifically for their use.

Poor presentation can contribute to your media release being placed in the 'round filing cabinet' on the floor. Your press release should be immediately recognisable as such and have the words 'press release', 'media release' or 'news release' in bold at the top. Your identity should also be easily determined, with a large, clear letterhead at the top of your page. You may wish to suggest a headline, but if you do, keep it under five words to give it any chance of being used. A one- or two-word identifier (known as a slug) is there to give the editor an instant idea of what the story is about, and for easy identification. Next should come an embargo date if you have one, or the words 'For immediate release' if you do not. Double-space your copy and provide large margins. This space allows for any changes, and for the subeditors to put information on the page (such as the page number for the story, if it is going in a box).

The most important information on your press release should be the very last line in bold at the bottom, which has the name and the phone numbers of the person to contact for extra information about the story. Ensure that this person is authorised to talk on the issue, and is available. The after-hours number is the most important, because often the story is not reached until later in the afternoon or evening. You may also supply information regarding photograph or visual opportunities at this point.

Figure 9.1 is a good example of a press release in terms of structure, content and presentation.

GETTING HELP

Usually you will send your media release on the facsimile (fax) machine, and for this reason it is recommended you keep it to one page. Hundreds of pages come through the machine every day, and, if someone is not monitoring it constantly, pages can easily get mixed up or go astray. It is also highly unlikely that they will use any more than one page, and if they do want a longer story the editor will assign a journalist to follow up your lead. Other modes of communication worth considering include e-mail, which is becoming increasingly popular with editors, or simply supplying your information on disc.

The best advice for anyone planning to work with the media is to make contact with journalists and to develop these contacts. Your contact may well be the news editor, chief of staff or the editor. Develop a list of contacts, just as journalists do. It is useful to ask their advice about dealing

MEDIA RELEASE

For immediate release
WORLD FIRST IN WINE

The world's first sparkling wine that never loses its bubbles has been released in Australia.

Fine Wines Inc. developed 'Sparkler' in conjunction with three national scientists.

Product manager, Paul Drink, said 'Sparkler' was the result of five years of intensive research and development.

'Where other wines lose their bubbles, sometimes within minutes, 'Sparkler' just keeps bubbling,' Mr Drink said.

'The input from the scientists was essential in determining the precise quantities of yeast to achieve continuous bubbles.'

'Sparkler' will be released throughout Australia this month, followed by a major export campaign.

End

**For more information and photographs contact..............
............; ph:...............(work); ph:..................(after hours);
e-mail address...................; fax..................**

Figure 9.1   An example of a press release

with the media. Some newspapers even offer free training courses for regular contributors.

If you are providing a press release on specialist information or special-interest material such as for the financial section, you will need to contact the appropriate section editor. For instance, many newspapers have a weekly real estate guide, with its own editor, journalists, photographers and advertising representatives. There are also magazines that aim carefully at a select group of readers and will require different content, style and lead time (the time the story is needed prior to printing). These requirements can be obtained by contacting the editor or news editor.

CHECKLIST FOR PRODUCING A PRESS RELEASE

☐ What do you hope to achieve with your press release—information, publicity or defence? Have you written it with this in mind?

☐ Have you applied the 'who cares principle'? What is the news angle and have you put it in the lead?

☐ Is the news 'hidden' or is it right at the start of the lead?

☐ Did you apply the ABC of journalism—accuracy, brevity and conciseness?

☐ Have you answered the 5Ws and H—who, what, when, where, why and how? Check particularly that the venue and time are included.

☐ Are all editorial comments removed except when attributed to someone? Have you given the source's full title and name?

☐ Have you removed all unnecessary adjectives?

☐ Is your suggested headline concise and descriptive?

☐ Have you checked your spelling—particularly of names?

☐ Has someone else proofread for spelling and factual errors?

☐ Are your words clear and familiar? Avoid jargon. Remember the KISS theory.

☐ Have you checked the presentation of your press release for all the essentials, including letterhead and embargo date—but particularly for the after-hours phone number?

FURTHER READING

Mathews, I. 1991. *How to Use the Media in Australia*. Penguin Books, Harmondsworth.

Hunt, T. and Grunig, J.E. 1994. *Public Relations Techniques*. Harcourt Brace College Publishers, Fort Worth, TX.

10

Promotional kits

Promotional kits are used for a variety of reasons by private and public organisations. They have been around for a long time and have been used to meet communication objectives in a range of ways, from promoting specific products to providing information on issues or events.

The product-specific promotional kit usually contains a variety of items, many discussed and explained elsewhere in this book. Most communication professionals would be involved in developing the promotional kits for use by the media on which this chapter focuses. These promotional kits contain standard information, such as media releases and backgrounders, but you can vary the contents of each piece of information to suit your event or issue.

Promotional kits are used to promote:

- new products
- films
- videos
- services

- events
- specific information
- issues.

The situations in which you use a promotional kit are limited only by your imagination, and so are the packaging and contents. However, you will always need to consider the audience you are preparing it for as well as the amount of time and money your organisation has to devote to the kit.

WHAT DO PROMOTIONAL KITS DO?

Promotional kits usually provide detailed information on whatever topic they cover, and often form a strategy of part of a wider campaign. For example, if you worked for a wildlife organisation and you were running a save-the-whale campaign, you might use a promotional kit to get information to journalists about your campaign. However, this may be only one part of your campaign, which might include public rallies, advertising and letter-writing. In this instance your promotional kit would contain some information on whales as well as the history of your save-the-whale campaign. It would also cover the latest developments in your campaign and statistics on the number of whales culled each year, and some details about various whale species. There would then be a section of material devoted specifically to your campaign, with information on the campaign's aims and objectives and what action is being taken provided through press releases, backgrounders and even brochures. In this instance, the brochure would probably be something your organisation has developed for other purposes, containing information about your organisation and its work.

You need again to keep the audience in mind when preparing a kit. There is no sense overloading the kit with information if your audience is a group of journalists, who have limited time and less inclination to read great reams of material. It would be better to provide short, simple fact sheets and a media release outlining the latest developments in your campaign. You could include other backup material, particularly for magazines or feature-writers who have more time to research and read, but most journalists probably will not read or use the information. You might need to develop a standard package that you distribute to the majority of journalists, and then add information to it for specific audiences such as the feature journalist or environmental roundsperson.

RANGE

The type of promotional kit—from the cover it comes in to its contents—will often depend on how much money you have to spend. There is usually not much point in going overboard with information and issue kits, but if you are launching a new perfume or a new toy it may be worth spending some extra money to present an innovative kit. For example, one cosmetics company chose to promote new products to the female youth market using a promotional kit. What was different about this kit was the unique use of a handbag shape to contain the cosmetic samples and information the company was distributing to young women.

Using unique approaches to the packaging of your promotional kit, particularly for one focusing on new products, is a great idea. Do not forget that the kit should reflect your organisation. So the wildlife organisation, for example, would probably use a recycled cardboard cover for the kit and recycled paper inside it, because it is an environmentally conscious organisation, while a perfume company would probably go for glossy covers with several colours because the kit is part of its image-creation strategy.

CONTENTS

Promotional kits usually come in a cardboard folder. These folders can either be specifically designed and made for the particular product or issue you are promoting, or you can predesign a folder that can be used to contain all of your promotional material. Keep a stock of these predesigned and printed folders on hand in case you have to prepare a promotional kit at short notice. If you have plenty of time and some money to spend, designing a special folder is a great way of housing the bits and pieces of information needed for a promotional kit. However, if your kit is for journalists, the housing will have little effect on them.

Contents include:

- cover folders
- contents list
- media releases
- photos
- flyers
- posters
- biographies
- chairman's messages
- information sheets
- backgrounders
- contact lists
- stickers/balloons
- product samples.

PREPARATION

When you have decided to prepare a promotional kit you will need to undertake some research, focusing on your target audience. Make sure you identify the various groups that make up your target audience, because you might have to vary the contents of the promotional kit for each of these groups. Think about what the audience needs—that is, what information they require and what information you want to get across to them. The most important aspect of this background research is identifying what your organisation wants to achieve through the promotional kit.

Once you have undertaken this basic research, you will need to start outlining the contents of the promotional kit and identifying the staff members in your organisation who have the skills to produce these items. Sometimes you, as the communication professional, will be responsible for producing the entire contents of the promotional kit, but there may be other people in your organisation who can assist. Find out as much as possible about the issue that you are promoting. Each separate piece of information in the kit should fulfil its own communication objective. Do not include information that does not meet a specific communication objective or contribute to the communication of the central issue.

Make sure the pieces of information you include are contained in suitable formats. For example, if you are including a media release, make sure it covers the news aspect of your issue. Do not include background information as a news release; use it as a backgrounder (see Chapter 12).

DISTRIBUTION

Most promotional kits would be distributed at press conferences or through the post. However, in recent years product promotional kits have been given out at a variety of venues, including nightclubs, train stations, shopping centres, entertainment venues, in fact, anywhere that target audiences congregate. This is a great way of promoting a new product, particularly if you have free samples to give away, but it will not always work for promotional kits focusing on issues or information. These kinds of kits are usually distributed to media organisations.

If you work in a small area, with, say, six media outlets, you can hand-deliver the promotional kit. It might then pay to phone the day before and organise an appointment with the chief of staff or a journalist, where you can sit down and take them through the material and explain the event or issue. If you work in a larger area, say a capital city, you will probably have to post the kit. If this is the case, call and make sure the media outlet has received your kit; the phone call can double as a way of drawing attention to your issue. Newsrooms get thousands of faxes and letters each day, so make sure that yours stands out and provides newsworthy information. An even better idea is to find out the names of reporters who cover the area of your issue and send the information to them directly. If you mail the kit, you will need to consider how much time to allow for the kit to arrive through the post and see that it is sent in time.

GETTING HELP

Sometimes it pays to get help the first time you have to produce a kit. There is a range of options for obtaining assistance with the design and content of promotional kits. Public relations companies will usually have someone who can provide these services. What they actually do for you will depend on the amount of help you need. You will always have to provide them with basic ideas about what you want the kit to contain and the information that will form the basis of the kit. Other sources of assistance include the freelance editor or writer, who can produce backgrounders, media releases, information sheets, biographies and other pieces of writing normally included in promotional kits.

PRINTING

Once the materials for your kit have been designed you may need to get the entire kit, including covers and inserts, printed by a professional printing firm. If you are going to distribute only a dozen kits, it might not be economical to have the kits printed, and photocopying is a cheaper alternative. However, photocopied promotional kits do not have the same impact or overall effect that can be achieved by a well-printed kit. Another inexpensive option is to use laser-printed originals.

If you decide to have your kit professionally printed, you will need to give the printer plenty of advance warning. It usually takes about 10 days from lodgment of artwork and proofs before the job is printed and ready to collect. Some printers may be able to shorten this time, while others might need longer. Make sure you check out the ability of printers in your area. Talk to them when you first start your job and regularly during the year, so that you know their requirements. This will help to avoid stress when you are rushing to get a promotional kit designed, written and printed in a short time. Make sure you provide a written outline of your requirements and that you get a signed and dated quote for your printing job. You will have to specify ink colours, paper type and colour, as well as the number of copies you need and, most importantly, the date and time you want to collect or have the final printed job delivered.

SCALDS PREVENTION CAMPAIGN—HOT WATER BURNS LIKE FIRE

This kit was aimed at health promotion officers. The organisation that distributed it expected the health promotion officers to work with communication and public relations officers to distribute it to local media and promote the issue to the public. Contents of this kit included:

- folder
- contents page
- facts on scalds
- activity suggestions for the community
- guide to scalds-prevention devices
- home safety checklist
- suggestions for scald-safer homes
- safe as houses brochure
- campaign activity summary
- reference material
- blank letterhead pages—for local activities.

CHECKLIST FOR PROMOTIONAL KITS

☐ Do you have a theme?
☐ Have you identified the information your kit must contain?
☐ Does each piece of information contribute to your theme?
☐ Have you assembled all the necessary items?
☐ Do you have a media release and a backgrounder?
☐ Have you supplied contact numbers for the media?
☐ Do you have an up-to-date distribution list?
☐ Have you followed up with media outlets to ensure they have received your kit?

FURTHER READING

Daniels, Tom D. and Spiker, Barry K. 1994. *Perspectives on Organizational Communication.* Brown & Benchmark, Dubuque, IA.

Hunt, Todd and Grunig, James E. 1994. *Public Relations Techniques.* Harcourt Brace College Publishers, Fort Worth, TX.

11

Video scripts

In some ways, writing scripts for videos requires the same skills that could be said to characterise any writing task. For a start, you need to identify (a) what you are required to do—that is, what function your work is meant to serve, and (b) the main ideas or arguments you are supposed to be communicating.

You need to know whether your script is meant:

- to argue a case (e.g. as to why your client should receive the accreditation their organisation is seeking from a professional standards body);
- to provide information (to potential clients or employees about how an organisation runs, and what its main achievements or areas of expertise are);
- to promote an upcoming event (once Sydney was given the 2000 Olympics, one of the first things the organising committee did was to commission a video that could be used to promote the event to a worldwide audience); or
- to recruit staff to an organisation.

The first, and most important, part of preparing to write your script involves consulting your client in a careful and detailed way. This may seem obvious, but it is amazing how often script writers pay only lip service to this part of their work: after all, they are the professionals, they know how to write the scripts; what can the clients tell them?

The answer is that, while script writers know how to write, it is the clients who know—or should know:

- what they want,
- the audience being addressed, and
- the field of activity that the video is going to be a part of and will be operating in.

THE AUDIENCE

The last point above is particularly important. One approach to selling, promoting, informing or arguing will not always work across different fields of activity. Colourful language and brash and bold statements might work in some fields—say, in a recruitment video for the army—but try using the same approach for recruiting accountants, or trying to gain accreditation for your client university from a very proper and serious-minded social welfare accreditation committee. The kind of language that works in one field sometimes automatically disqualifies you from serious consideration in another.

You will not always know the field you are going to be working in, so you need to do plenty of research to bring yourself up to speed. Your clients should be your first port of call. After all, they are the ones who know what they want. Or do they?

You need to work that out with them. If they are clear and focused, they will be able to give you specific advice as to what they want, who they want it from, and the best ways (the types of language and arguments needed) to achieve it. If they are not focused, it is part of your job to help them.

To take one example: the Sydney 2000 Olympics video was a dud, and you have been asked to come up with a different one. You ask the organising committee what they want, and they say, predictably enough, 'to promote the Sydney 2000 Olympics'. But is that the case and, if it is, is it enough?

The answer is no! There is a lot more to it than that. First, you need to redefine the task. Part of your job will be to promote the Olympics, but you are promoting Sydney (and Australia) as much as anything. If you were merely promoting the Olympics, you might write about handball, the triple jump and Greco-Roman wrestling. This is all very well if your audience is made up of Greco-Romans who would do anything to watch people jumping into sandpits. If you want to attract millions of Japanese, Scandinavian and American tourists who are looking for a holiday destination while taking in the Greco-Roman wrestling, you will want to write about the beaches, the Opera House, the climate, and just how safe and friendly the country is.

RESEARCH

If your clients cannot give you a focused task and audience, you must talk to them until you are confident that you know what is required. But your research has only just started.

We have suggested that foreign tourists might be attracted to the Sydney Olympics because of the beaches and other obvious attractions. But what if your clients decided that they wanted to aim this video at one particular group of tourists—say, Germans? You cannot presume that everybody is attracted to the same things. You might go off and do some research on the way Australia is perceived in Germany: it would be easy to do some library searches, to pick up some information on the Internet, or to check with the Australian Tourism Commision or the German Consulate about what aspects of Australia seem to be of interest to Germans. If your research told you that Aboriginal culture—say, Aboriginal music or art—was popular, you might want to include some specific references to that culture in your written text that would allow for the use of Aboriginal images in the video.

There is a lot more research you might want to do, or points you need clarified. Is the video meant merely to get people to come for the Olympics, or are you hoping to attract people to stay on after the games are finished? Are you selling Sydney, New South Wales, or Australia? You need to identify and research these questions by talking to your clients and gathering enough information so that you know just exactly what your task is before you start writing.

PRESENTATION AND STRUCTURE

Set out your script in a simple, user-friendly way. The type should be large and double-spaced for ease of reading. Remember to leave space where you want visuals without any verbals.

When structuring your script, apply the 'primacy/recency' principle: people generally remember what they hear 'first' and 'last'. Start with something (appropriately) catchy and arresting, continue with your main theme, and then try to finish with something particularly memorable—similar to your introduction. To avoid losing your audience between introduction and conclusion you need constantly to vary the pace. You can do this by alternating between the presenter talking to the camera and voice-overs or graphics.

THE SCRIPT

A great deal of work has been done on how many ideas an audience can take in during a speech or talk, and it is generally felt that one new idea every five minutes is enough to tax even the most intelligent audience. And after 10 minutes a large percentage of the audience will not be paying much attention anyway. Something similar applies to audiences of your video. Ten minutes is probably the longest you want to run, which means that you will be able to deal with only a couple of ideas; the rest of your time is going to be taken up with examples, or repeating your main points.

Ten minutes of video translates into 800 words. After all, 80 words a minute is equivalent to a normal conversational pace, and there is no point in racing through a block of information if it means that the audience cannot keep up, or will not take the trouble to follow what is being said. Eighty words a minute is slow enough to allow easy comprehension, but not so slow as to induce sleep.

VISUALS

Despite all that, your script should not add up to 800 words, because video is predominantly a visual medium. Yes, your script is important, but the audience will probably pay more attention to the visuals. Anyway, most videos are characterised by stretches during which the images do the work: think of how (in)effective your Sydney Olympics video would be if you only talked about—rather than showed—the Opera House or an Aboriginal painting. As a general rule, it is best to devote a third of your run time to some kind of verbal content; this means that your visuals will still carry the video, but your verbal script will help your audience to make sense of—or contextualise—your images.

The main point to remember is that you should not try to compete with strong visuals: the pictures will win every time.

So you are faced with having to write between the main images, coming in only when there is need for specific information or a narrative of some kind. Of course the length of your script will vary depending on the extent to which your video requires a continuous narrative—but while your reader will be speaking at around 80 words a minute, they will not be speaking all the time.

Let us presume that in a 10-minute video on the Sydney Olympics you end up with a script of 300 words. That is not many words, but remember that you want to make only a couple of main points anyway. What structure should you use?

Keep things as simple as possible: people will not give you their attention if they have to work too hard. Start with a simple introduction that encapsulates the main point or function of the video—something like this:

In June in the year 2000 the world's attention will be on Sydney, when it hosts the next Olympic Games. That's probably enough reason to book your flight to Sydney now—but that's only the beginning of Sydney's attractions.

What this introduction does is to catch your attention (the glamour of the 2000 Olympics) and then make use of it ('while I have your attention, let's tell you a few other things about Sydney'). Remember, you have enough time and words to get through a couple of ideas.

You are targeting middle- to late-middle-aged English tourists. You have done your research, and everything indicates that two issues are particularly important—beaches (nothing too dramatic: paddling rather than surfing beaches), and safety.

One final, important point to bear in mind when you are choosing visuals is the question of copyright and artistic credit. Do not just assume that you can use certain visuals: you need to find out if they are available and what they cost, and you have to credit them.

COMBINING VISUAL AND VERBAL

Perhaps the most difficult task you will face is to come up with a mix of visuals and verbals that work together, rather than distracting attention from each other. The first point to remember is that if the visuals you are using are sufficiently arresting and self-explanatory, leave them alone! There is nothing worse than having an inappropriate voice-over get in the way if the viewer is taken in by the visuals. If you are making your points through visuals, your verbal or written text should guide and contextualise—but never dominate.

Generally speaking, you should let your visuals do the work. However, there are occasions—particularly with videos, where the main function is to provide specific and perhaps detailed information—where you need a strong written or verbal text. If you are arguing for a particular program to be accredited, or relating information about the services an institution provides, you do not just want to leave an impression—you want to convince or inform.

Whether you use voice-overs, have someone appear on the video, or use written text, will again depend on the kind of video you are making. To give you an example: if you are scripting a video for an accreditation, then the accrediting body will want to see and hear from the people running the program—particularly senior staff, or staff with particular expertise. Shots of buildings and palm trees will not work here.

The beauty of a written text is that it combines the visual with the specific, guiding details of the verbal. Do not overuse written text, or you may as well just produce a brochure or a booklet. Use text if you want to signal clearly a change of direction or emphasis, and to reiterate important points.

Language

Verbal and written texts are not mere adjuncts to visuals, then: they can often communicate your main points. But how do you write about those points? Using the simplest language possible. Not because your audience does not have good 'Australian', but because, no matter what your audience, your language should be easy to comprehend:

> Sydney has some of the most beautiful, and safest, beaches in the world. There are few more relaxing experiences than lying back on a beach chair at Manly

in 25 degrees Celsius, soaking up the sun and watching the world go by.

This might sound simple—even simplistic—but it is easy to listen to. Anyway, in this case the visuals should be doing most of the work: you are merely helping them along.

Once you have made your points (about beaches and safety), repeat them! Why? Because you want your audience to come away with those two ideas, and the more you make your points, the more likely it is that your audience will retain them.

How can you repeat your ideas without boring your audience? After all, you cannot just keep writing the same sentences over and over again. What you can do, however, is to make use of, and repeat, certain key words or their synonyms. You might want to make the point that a Sydney holiday will be, above all else, a relaxing holiday, and you can achieve this by using words such as 'easy-going', 'lazy', 'snooze, 'lie back', as well as 'relaxed'.

Now we explain how you would go about getting a video script written. We have considered this from two perspectives:

1. We look at what steps you need to take if you are contracting the writing of the script out partially or wholly to a professional scriptwriter (working for, say, a local television station or a video production house).
2. We assess the work required if you are going to write the script yourself.

TO CONTRACT OUT OR DO IT YOURSELF?

There are a number of reasons why you might choose to contract the writing of your script out to a media group or production company.

- You will probably end up with a more professional and effective product.

- Your script should be finished more quickly; this is important if you have a tight deadline.
- It frees up your own time: learning to write a video script 'on the job' is likely to be a time-consuming process. You probably have better things to do.

On the other hand, you might decide to write your own script if:

- you simply do not have the money to bring in professionals, and/or
- the material and project you are working on is not easily understood by or explicable to outsiders (e.g. if it involves the communication of predominantly technical information), and
- you have such a tight schedule that bringing outsiders up to speed is out of the question.

How to contract out

If you have decided that you want to contract the writing of the script, partially or wholly, out to professionals, there are a number of stages you need to go through.

1. Contact your local television station or check in the *Yellow Pages* for video production houses. You will find plenty of companies offering their services: scan their advertisements and see which ones seem most appropriate to your needs. For instance, if you need a video script for a recruitment drive for your company, or to get a course accredited for a TAFE college, there is not much point in contacting companies that do only weddings and reunions. Your local television station is a likely bet because it will probably have staff with experience in writing videos for corporate, industrial and training purposes.

2. Once you have contacted a number of companies, compare what they offer in terms of cost and time. You must approach this decision with the constraints of your budget

in mind, but you also have a deadline. Get at least three quotes, and weigh up the cost of those quotes against the projected completion dates you have been given before making a decision.

3. When you have made your choice, work as closely as possible with the script writers. Start by giving them a rough idea of what your video is meant to achieve, its context, and the target audience(s). The more specific information you provide, the better the script and the shorter the writing time.

4. To make sure everything runs as smoothly as possible, provide the script writers with
   - an abstract (of a few hundred words) outlining what the video is meant to achieve;
   - the correct titles and names of all the people involved;
   - names and phone or fax numbers of any other sources of information.

5. Next, you should consult the script writers about music, visuals and graphics. If you can supply any of these, it will cut time and costs. Unless you know what you are doing, you could be making it more difficult for the script writers.

6. If you supply materials such as graphics or music, you need to get permission to use these from the copyright owners. This is important, because some material is expensive to get permission for, and could blow your budget.

7. Do not leave the script writers to their own devices. You do not want to get in the way once you have contracted them, but you should check regularly on their progress. You should not wait until everything is finished to discover that they have got it completely wrong. Schedule progress meetings, during which they can explain what they are doing and what materials or extra information they require.

CHECKLIST FOR VIDEO SCRIPTS

☐ Always begin by clarifying what it is you are required to do—who is your audience, and what does your client want of them?

☐ Equally importantly, research the field you are writing to and about. You need to be aware of the kinds of language and approaches that are suited to the field you are dealing with.

☐ Work out just how much of a script is required. Should there be a continuous narrative or plenty of information, or do you just need to work with your visuals?

☐ Identify the purpose of the video in your introduction: make sure the audience gets the message at the beginning.

☐ Try to start with something that is punchy and arresting, remembering that, if your task is a 'serious' one (gaining accreditation), being too punchy could be a disadvantage.

☐ Identify a couple of ideas, and make sure you follow them through in your script.

☐ Repeat your main ideas, using key words and synonyms.

☐ Use simple, straightforward language.

If you are contracting the script out:

☐ Get three quotes.

☐ Provide an abstract, and the names and numbers of people involved.

☐ Consult about music, visuals and graphics.

☐ Make copyright arrangements.

☐ Check regularly with the script writer.

FURTHER READING

Wilcox, D. et al. 1992. *Public Relations: Strategies and Tactics.* HarperCollins, New York.

PART III

Presentations and events

12

Backgrounders

Backgrounders are used in media and promotional kits, and in information packages provided to government or business officials and organisations. They provide additional contextual information—of a kind that is not normally found in media releases—on issues of public interest, particularly 'sensitive' issues (such as government policy changes that might lead to widespread redundancies in an industry or locality) that involve, or may have impact on, your organisation.

Two critical points about backgrounders are:

- They have to provide enough information so that readers can make sense of and grasp 'where' an issue came from (its history, the twists and turns of its development, the various contexts that inform it).
- At the same time they must provide that contextual information selectively and in a condensed form, of no more than a couple of pages in length; the reader needs

thorough background information that can be accessed quickly and by a non-specialist.

The first function of backgrounders, then, is to bring the reader up to speed on an issue in a condensed and accessible form. But there is a second, and equally important function that follows from the first, and that is: to communicate to outside bodies how these issues may develop, the possible ramifications of such developments, and your organisation's likely responses. This is much more difficult to achieve than the first function. Remember, the effectiveness of a backgrounder depends, to a great extent, on it being seen as thorough, factual and neutral. However, when backgrounders are dealing with potential developments, their credibility will depend on the extent to which these developments can logically and reasonably be connected to past contexts. They are not meant to be 'position papers', but summaries of current or potential 'facts'.

What kinds of organisation use backgrounders, and in what circumstances?

- A public health authority spokesperson might have to produce a backgrounder about what steps the authority was taking to combat the outbreak of a new disease.
- A government department might have to provide a backgrounder about a politician visiting a public authority or private company to open a building or to preside over the formal commencement of a new initiative or venture.
- A private company might produce a backgrounder in order to address questions about an industrial dispute involving the organisation.

Backgrounders differ from most other forms of professional writing in two related ways:

- they need to be as factual as you can make them, and
- they should be written in a neutral style.

In other words, backgrounders are not meant to be persuasive, emotional, rhetorical or personalised. The extent to which they are effective largely depends not on persuasive language or striking examples but on the writer's research skills, and the extent to which that research has been deployed with thoroughness and clarity.

RESEARCH

If you are going to produce a document that is thorough and accurate, and therefore credible, you will need to do a considerable amount of painstaking research. Remember, no one source or information medium is going to be enough. It makes sense to research in the obvious places—newspapers, for instance, as well as relevant journals—but these will cover only some of the ground. The best way to approach the question of research is to identify, and if necessary to contact, any group or individual (politicians, government departments, businesses, pressure groups) that might have an involvement or a stake in the issue. This will help in two ways:

- This kind of research will broaden the base of your enquiries; stakeholders will be more likely to have a comprehensive knowledge of who is involved in an issue, and what communications they have produced.
- By talking to stakeholders you should be able to get a better grasp of the different contexts which will help to focus your research.

GENRE AND STYLE

Backgrounders must be complete, accurate and continually updated: in other words, they have to present the reader with the who, what, where, when, how and why of an issue. For clarity's sake, that information should generally be in chronological order, with a statement about the main issues at the beginning, followed by details of the main contexts, the current situation, and potential developments.

Finally, backgrounders need clearly to identify both the organisation that is preparing the backgrounder and any sources that have been used to provide contextual information. What is required is:

- the name of the organisation
- a contact name and numbers (phone, fax, e-mail)
- a referencing system that is consistent, clearly differentiates information that has been taken direct from another source, and is easy to follow.

WRITING BACKGROUNDERS

There are two important points about the writing style required for backgrounders:

- The narrative has to do all the work: you cannot expect the reader to make connections, or to separate different bits of information.
- The narrative should be written in the present tense.

How do you do all the work for your readers? There are a number of ways:

- Each section should be brief—no more than a few paragraphs.
- Indicate the relationship between different sections. For instance, if you are writing about how a set of trade figures eventually gave rise to a government review that resulted in new policies, you must clearly signal, in your narrative, the causal relationship between these events.

Why should you write in the present tense? Because a backgrounder is meant to provide an overview from a particular time—the present—of what brought us to this point, and where we might go from here. The emphasis should be on what all this information means for the current situation.

Backgrounders and contexts

What kinds of contexts should you include in backgrounders? You should be as thorough as possible, and make reference to anything that might have had, or might yet have, a bearing on an issue. The kinds of contexts that are normally referred to are:

- social (a locality, town or age group may be facing massive job losses);
- legislative (what laws have applied, and how they have changed);
- political (what positions politicians and political parties have taken on an issue).

Other contexts (e.g. historical and environmental) should be included if relevant.

Current circumstances

Backgrounders have to show:

- how and why the present situation came about; also
- the policy, political, social and/or historical options that were available, and were not taken, and the rationale for making one set of decisions and not another.

Potential developments

This is the most difficult aspect of backgrounders to bring off, because there is the requirement to remain neutral and factual while positing 'what might happen'. The following areas need to be covered:

- There should be reference to possible changes to or developments of the current situation.
- There should be reference to the potential impact (again social, political, environmental) of such developments.

- There should be a list of the different ways in which your organisation is likely to respond to these potential changes.

If the effectiveness of any backgrounder depends on thoroughness, factuality and clarity, how can a backgrounder be effective when it is in essence trying to predict the future? There are two main responses to this point.

First, you need to ensure that your potential scenarios, and their concomitant impact, have as much credibility as possible. The best way to do this is to make use of the most authoritative and disinterested sources. There is not much credibility in simply plucking a few possibilities out of the air and pretending that they are factual.

On the other hand, Professor Smith, with a long history of research in this area, or the chairperson of a company that is closely involved in decision-making, or a senator chairing a government review committee, all have status and credibility, either as experts or as insiders. If you make reference to what these people have said and the predictions they have made, your suggestions are likely to be more convincing. You can add to that sense of conviction by referring to statistics, and to the patterns and trends that can be found in those statistics.

Second, you can add to the credibility of your suggested scenarios through the thoroughness and accuracy of the information you have provided about past contexts.

DOCUMENTATION

Generally, there is no point in including a considerable body of source material in a backgrounder. Given that you want to keep the amount of information your reader needs to get through to a minimum, adding piles of documentation will only detract from your purpose. However, we have already pointed out that references to credible or authoritative sources will increase the credibility of your backgrounder, so how do you make use of these sources without providing too much material for your reader?

First, you should append any document or source that is absolutely essential reading, preferably with your own brief summary of the document attached. Second, you need clearly and accurately to reference all the sources you have used, as well as any other sources that might be relevant. This is to allow your readers both to check the accuracy of your information and to pursue, in more detail, points you have alerted them to.

In deciding on a reference style, you should be guided by the need to provide your reader with easy access to the source. There are a number of conventional referencing styles that can be used for printed material, but you may find yourself needing to reference material other than print documents (e.g. film documentaries, speeches, or sources on the Internet). If in doubt, consult your local library; it will be able to provide you with referencing styles for both print and non-print material.

Figure 12.1 is an example of a backgrounder.

UPDATING

As we have stressed all along, the effectiveness of a backgrounder depends on your ability to explain, concisely and thoroughly, what the situation is at the time, how and why it got to this stage, and likely developments. A backgrounder loses credibility if the 'now' it puts forward turns out to be 'then'—in other words, if your information is not up to date. The best way to update a backgrounder is to go back to the sources you used to get your information (a journal, a government committee, a library, the Internet) and see what new information is available. The accuracy of your 'future scenarios' will depend on your ability to update as often as possible—at the very least, just before it is sent out each time.

You should also check how useful your readers are finding the material; they can alert you to issues and contexts that are not covered, or to questions about the validity or accuracy of your information.

Bedrock Uni opts for fees

Bedrock University has decided that from 1999 it will offer places in its undergraduate programs to full fee paying local students.

Local student and academic staff groups have criticised the move as a step towards the introduction of a user-pays system in tertiary education, and have threatened to campaign against it.

Local students who are accepted into tertiary institutions do not pay up-front fees, but are required to contribute to the Higher Education Contribution Scheme (HECS), after completing their course and commencing work. The deductions from their salary commence at a threshold of $23,000, and the amount they are required to pay depends on the course they have taken.

Undergraduate tertiary places are available to full fee paying overseas students.

The opportunity to reserve undergraduate places for full fee paying local students came about when the Federal Government changed the policy this year. The Education Minister, Senator Loadstone, has indicated that the change in policy was meant to encourage institutions to rely less on government funding.

Five universities (out of thirty-two nationwide) have decided to reserve places for local full fee paying undergraduate students. Professor Rich, Vice-Chancellor at Summit University, said "the move would allow universities to raise extra revenue needed to compensate for reduced government funding, but would not disadvantage ordinary HECS students" (*Australian*, 21/7/97, p. 32).

Student and staff unions have staged demonstrations at all the universities where this decision has been taken, but all thirty-two universities are likely to accept this opportunity by 1999.

Student and staff protests are likely to continue, but indications are that they will (reluctantly) accept the move. Greg Arrias, President of the National Tertiary Student Union, recently wrote that "while it looks like most universities will embrace this change, we still have strong reservations, and will monitor universities to ensure HECS students are not disadvantaged" (*Australian*, 23/7/97, p. 3).

Figure 12.1 An example of a backgrounder

CHECKLIST FOR BACKGROUNDERS

☐ Include all relevant information, including the names of organisations, dates, contact names and numbers.
☐ Append any relevant documentation.
☐ Clearly and accurately reference all sources.
☐ Update your material.

FURTHER READING

Hunt, T. and Grunig, J. 1994. *Public Relations Techniques.* Harcourt Brace, Fort Worth, TX.

13

Briefing notes

Briefing notes are similar, in some ways, to backgrounders. The main difference is that briefing notes have a more specific and immediate function, and there is normally little time to prepare them.

The main function of briefing notes is to provide an organisational spokesperson, at reasonably short notice, with sufficient background material to deal with questions on a particular issue. For instance, a story breaks that a company is involved in a business venture that appears to have raised the ire of environmental groups, and a news conference is scheduled in a few hours' time. The company representative will be expected to have a firm grasp of the issue and its contexts, and to anticipate and answer questions from a variety of parties—including some that might be hostile and aggressive. The credibility of the company will depend, to a large extent, on how well the spokesperson presents the company's position and can satisfactorily answer or deflect questions.

The first point about writing successful briefing notes is to have either a file of relevant material to call on or immediate access to sources of information. Normally, professional writers working for an organisation will have files on major projects and activities, including background histories and names of contact persons. In other words, when you are suddenly presented with the task of providing briefing for a spokesperson, you should either have the information available at your fingertips or know who can give it to you.

What kind of information should be provided? Anything that will help the spokesperson negotiate a question or interrogation session. This includes:

- a description of the issue;
- the history;
- the nature of the organisational involvement;
- the main problems or controversy;
- the type of question session being held (news conference, delegation, protest);
- the groups or individuals the spokesperson will be talking to;
- of those attending, which groups are likely to be supportive or hostile;
- the kinds of questions that will be asked, and possible answers to those questions.

Again, as with backgrounders, you should provide enough information, while giving the reader (who may have little or no familiarity with the issue) a reasonable chance of taking it in and at least appearing to be on top of the issue. Figure 13.1 is an example of briefing notes.

How comprehensive does the information need to be? This depends on the situation the spokesperson is in. If a press conference has been scheduled with a variety of interested parties (say, 'green' groups wanting to know about the organisation's environmental record) attending, as well as news organisations, then the spokesperson will need both specific and general information. If the spokesperson is

Issue
The State Government has decided that from next year the elective surgery waiting list will be cut by up to 20%.

Developments
The Medical Association, the Nursing Union and the Pensioners' Association have threatened to mount a media campaign against the move.

Meeting
The Minister is to meet a delegation representing the three groups on 25 November at 3 pm in his office.

Organisations Involved
There will be a representative from the Medical Association, the Nursing Union and the Pensioners' Association.

Areas of Concern
These groups feel that a 20% cut constitutes a serious erosion of services that will cause hardship to low income earners and the elderly. They want to be consulted about the planned cut. They have threatened a publicity campaign, and may take industrial action. There have already been numerous negative responses, aired in the media, to the announcement.

Format of Meeting
The representatives will meet with the Minister for an hour to outline their case, question the Minister, and seek an undertaking that the decision will be reviewed and appropriate groups consulted.

Our Organisational Involvement
The Minister and the Department are responsible for formulating and implementing the decision.

Friends/Foes
Of the three groups represented, the Medical Association is not entirely antagonistic—they understand the need to cut elective surgery numbers. The Nursing Union and the Pensioners' Association are likely to be strongly oppositional.

Questions/Answers
The two most likely and important questions are:
Q1 What's the rationale for the cut?
Q2 What criteria will be used in making the cuts, and will the Minister consult relevant groups about the criteria?
Answers
A1 Hospital staff are overworked, and there is a shortage of space in the public system hospitals.
A2 Criteria will be decided after consultation with relevant groups.

Figure 13.1 Briefing notes

meeting a group or an individual asking about a single issue (say, what environmental impact measures the organisation has undertaken regarding this project), then too much history and background material will only get in the way.

How should briefing notes be written and set out? The short answer is:

- They should be characterised by straightforward, everyday, non-technical language.
- They should be in bulleted list form.
- The different types of information (history, names, organisational involvement and position) should be clearly differentiated through the use of headings and subheadings.

CHECKLIST FOR BRIEFING NOTES

Make sure you have provided the following information:

☐ a brief history of the issue, its contexts and controversies;

☐ the nature of your organisation's involvement;

☐ the type of question session, the groups attending, and their positions;

☐ questions that are likely to be asked.

FURTHER READING

Hunt, T. and Grunig, J. 1994. *Public Relations Techniques.* Harcourt Brace, Fort Worth, TX.

14

Conferences

Of all the tasks a professional communicator may have to undertake, organising conferences would have to be one of the most time-consuming and fraught with disaster. Conferences are a forum for the exchange of information and ideas, and can be used to discuss and 'workshop' a particular problem or area. There are usually a number of guest speakers and at least one key speaker. Often the keynote speaker will also be asked to act as raconteur (a role like master of ceremonies, but one in which the person sums up papers, suggests areas or themes for further discussion and orchestrates question time). There is generally a raconteur for conferences of half a day or one day in duration. For longer conferences, with many sessions running parallel over several days, numerous 'session chairs' will take on this role. Most organisations and industry bodies use the one-day forum, while educational institutions tend towards three, four and sometimes five-day conferences.

BENEFITS

A conference can produce results far beyond expectations, particularly in problem-solving sessions. It is an excellent opportunity for networking, which is generally the main benefit of such a forum. These contacts can prove to be extremely useful for participants and organisers. If well organised, a conference can also be great publicity for your organisation, particularly through word of mouth from happy participants.

DRAWBACKS

A lot of organisational time is required to ensure that a conference is smooth-running. It sounds extreme, but planning for most conferences should start at least a year in advance to ensure maximum attendance and minimum problems. Because planning involves a lot of people and many elements, disasters will occur. These range from key speakers missing their plane connection to dinner not turning up on time. Often it will mean organising not only a conference program but associated programs, including tours and inspections. You may also have to consider putting together a completely separate program for partners.

TRAVEL ARRANGEMENTS

If you are making the travel arrangements for guest or key speakers, be prepared to be flexible. You have chosen these speakers because they are experts in their particular fields. This also means very busy people who will require plenty of notice, and travel arrangements which can take this into account. Put everything in writing, and obtain written confirmation (by fax or e-mail) from the invited guests for any arrangements you make.

The best advice is to find patient and well-organised travel agents and let them look after this aspect of the conference. Accept that you cannot do everything, and surround yourself with people who can and will help.

THE VENUE

Pick somewhere easy to access, but preferably removed from everyone's workplace. For ease of organisation your own workplace would be ideal, but this also means that you (and other participants) are still accessible and might be interrupted by phone calls or taken away from the conference by 'emergencies'. Pick a resort, conference centre, hotel or university that has the facilities you require. Access to audiovisual equipment, photocopiers, computers (for speakers who have brought their papers on disk) and basics such as water, telephones and toilets should be on your list of musts for the venue. You should also consider disabled access and facilities for vision- or hearing-impaired participants.

THE CONTENT

The conference should have a theme or area of interest which will attract participants and speakers. This should be topical, have some currency and perhaps even a little controversy. For instance, 'Towards 2010' would be a good theme for any number of organisations including government, education, health and marketing groups. Problem-solving or strategic planning may be part of these events. Once you have established the theme of your conference you will know your target audience and can begin to promote the event. For instance, if the conference is on advances in laser equipment for cosmetic surgery, the audience is quite specific. Promotion can be targeted directly at suppliers and surgeons through avenues such as medical journals and newsletters aimed at these two groups. It may, in fact, be a case of a conference with only invited speakers, which for you is less problematic than an open event.

THE PROGRAM

The program is perhaps the most difficult aspect of conference organisation in terms of taking everyone's needs into account, particularly those of the guest speakers. The program is the main reason it is necessary to start early and to give participants a cut-off date far in advance of your own deadlines. Keynote speakers should also be given maximum notice. Make the call for papers your first task, as this will give you information on rough numbers, themes and session ideas. This also gives you details to start organising conference facilities, accommodation, catering and other requirements—though it should be noted that numbers will fluctuate in all directions before the final date.

Now is the time to organise the registration form. Check that everything is spelled out on the form, and, if participants are giving papers, ask after special requirements such as audiovisual equipment. The registration form should detail the key theme of the conference and any expected subthemes or groupings of interest. As stated earlier, you may have to include tours and inspections as part of the program and perhaps a day or half-day of sightseeing for participants. If you feel you should put together a separate program for accompanying persons, this is another job that should go to your competent travel agent. Double-check that details on the registration form such as dates, times and contact numbers are correct, not forgetting to allow for those who may want to arrive early or leave late.

CATERING

Perhaps the most vital aspect of any conference or function program is the catering. Food is certainly one of the most problematic areas: you must take into account varying tastes and needs (e.g. vegetarians), and ensure that you have a section on your registration form that highlights this. Talk to other people who have organised functions and find out who is the best caterer in the area. It is also a nice touch if specialities from the region can be incorporated in the menu, particularly for out-of-town visitors. Try for daytime meals that are light and healthy, with more complex menus for the evenings. This is because people will fall asleep after a heavy midday feast. One conference key speaker remarked that he was unsure whether it was a bad or a good omen that he had been scheduled to talk after lunch. He hoped it was a compliment on his ability to keep people awake!

TIMING

Three days seems to be the optimum time for a conference, with perhaps the bulk of the participants arriving the evening before to a special welcome function. If you are expecting any more than 50–60 participants, with the bulk of them giving papers, you will need at least three days. This is generally the case with academic conferences. A one-day conference is more common, and obviously a lot easier to organise. Do not make times for papers any shorter than 20 minutes (with 10 minutes for questions). Any less than this does not give people time even to summarise what they will be saying—let alone actually say it.

PEOPLE

You need to surround yourself with organised, patient, flexible people. The key speakers are an important choice, and should be sociable as well as knowledgeable, particularly if they are taking on the role of raconteur. They should also be able to deal with the media (as you undoubtedly would like to generate some publicity from the conference).

You need very gracious but ruthless people for raconteurs or session chairs. It is imperative that they stick to the program, even if it means cutting someone off in full flow. Speakers know the time limits, and if they are any good will have organised their papers accordingly.

The most important people, though, are the support staff. These are the people who will get phoned by participants wanting to know odd details, the people who will take messages for organisers and participants, the people who will photocopy last-minute papers, call doctors, fix overhead projectors, organise taxis etc.

Take care when choosing your travel agent, as a competent one will take a large load off your shoulders.

GETTING HELP

When it comes to conferences, one-stop shopping is best. Most accommodation houses these days include conference facilities and, better still, conference facilitators! It is then a matter of giving them all the details (i.e. dates, numbers, audiovisual and room requirements, the program with meal times, breaks and special needs) and leave it up to them. It will cost more this way, but less in time and headaches.

By the time you have coordinated all these separate elements the monetary savings will probably be small and your headache large. Look for someone with a proven track record in the field. Poach any ideas from other conferences. For instance, a conference registration form can ask for expressions of interest in being session chairs. This will give you a pool of people long before you are putting the program together. Figure 14.1 is an example of a conference registration form.

WORKING WITH THE MEDIA

International Association for Media Managers
hosted by Sunnyvale University, Sunnyvale
November 25 - November 29

The theme for the IAMM conference this year is Working With The Media, and aims to explore and encourage links between media relations managers and those in the journalism industry. Co-authored material and joint presentations are especially invited. Sunnyvale is a very popular international resort town, particularly at the time of our conference. In order to ensure we have accommodation, meals, transport and conference facilities for you, we need your assistance now. Please return this registration form (completed) with your payment to confirm your booking BEFORE September 1. We cannot guarantee accommodation if you reply after this date. Please complete the rest of this form (two pages) and circle your selections where appropriate.

Name and Title: ....
Organisation: ....
Address: ....
Telephone: ....
Fax: .... **E-mail:** ....

Full Conference Attendance (all costs are in US dollars).
The following includes bed and breakfast at Sunnyvale International Inn; all conference sessions including the welcome beach barbecue; conference dinner; and VIP passes to the Sunnyvale Casino.

* IAMM members - $700   * Twin share - $590
* Non-members - $850   * Twin share - $740

My partner will be attending - Yes/No (please see over for special offers for partners).

Additional nights accommodation
I require additional accommodation on: November 24 - Yes/No
                                              November 29 - Yes/No
Other (please detail): ....

I have special food requirements   Yes/No
If Yes, please detail any special requirements or allergies..
....

I have special presentation requirements   Yes/No
Please circle any of the following you may require for your presentation.
Overhead Projector   Powerpoint   Slide projector
Whiteboard   Flipchart   Video player/monitor
Other   Please give details..
I am willing to be a session chair during the conference   Yes/No

Don't forget to complete the other side of this form, and
DON'T FORGET YOUR SUNSCREEN!

Figure 14.1 A conference registration form

PREPROGRAM CONFERENCE CHECKLIST

☐ Organise the conference theme.
☐ Contact key speakers.
☐ Publicise the conference and call for papers.
☐ Set an early deadline for abstracts and registration forms.
☐ Ensure that registration forms include details such as special needs (food, disabilities) and session chair availability.
☐ Organise a conference venue (complete with conference convenor).
☐ Talk to a travel agent about your special needs.
☐ Arrange a meeting with all support staff.
☐ Collate abstracts and registration forms.
☐ Compile a draft program.

FURTHER READING

Baskin, O. and Aronoff, C. 1988 (2nd edn). *Public Relations: The Profession and the Practice.* Wm C. Brown, Dubuque, IA.

15

Press conferences

The best way to describe a press conference is as a 'bulk interview'. A press conference is a single time-efficient interview with many journalists instead of many individual interviews, and is used when a press release cannot convey all the necessary information. Generally the structure of a press or media conference is that the interviewee or speaker will give a summary of the information to be released and then allow time for questions. The time allowed may be anything from one minute to one hour.

A press conference is used for three major purposes:

- to release information,
- to promote a new organisation, service or product, or
- to defend the reputation of your organisation or yourself.

BENEFITS

The major benefit for anyone staging a press conference is that they have to conduct only one 'interview', instead of repeating the same interview with numerous journalists. It is an ideal method for conveying a lot of information quickly and easily. Because it is a managed event you can control the timing, duration and information released. As the press conference is for the media, your information will reach a large audience with little outlay or delay.

DRAWBACKS

The major drawback to press conferences is that journalists do not like them! The main problem in their eyes is that everyone gets to hear all the questions and all the answers. You can guarantee that journalists will try very hard to catch the interviewee on the way out for at least one 'individual' question and a potential 'scoop'. Journalists are also notorious when it comes to RSVPs—generally they do not. So it is up to you to chase, nag and cajole. The other major drawback is that, even if they have confirmed their attendance, this can change at any moment. You may have a particularly news-worthy press conference organised, but there is always the chance you will lose out to another story. For instance, you have planned a news conference that will be launched by the manager of your organisation, thus ensuring some quot-able quotes. However, as the media are heading to your venue they hear about a fire on the other side of town. Sorry, but the immediacy and impact of the fire story (not to mention the visuals) means that it will win every time. Also, although it is a managed event, if your speaker is unable to cope with a barrage by the media you will soon lose control.

CONTENT

Journalists have three main sources of news:

- regular events—rounds, meetings, shows;
- managed events—press conferences, launches, reviews; and
- spontaneous events—disasters, accidents, walk-ins.

Even though more than 70 per cent of the news in the media originates from managed events, press releases and leads from professional communicators, journalists tend to be cynical and suspicious of 'spin doctors' or people trying to 'manage' the media. For this reason you must go out of your way to ensure that the press conference is newsworthy and will pass the test when the editor is deciding whether to send a journalist or a camera crew to the event.

Try to combine a number of news angles or elements to attract the media. The Prime Minister's press secretary probably does not need to worry about this, nor do those working for the Royal Family, as generally whatever these VIPs do or say makes news. However, you need to come up with something to attract the media. A VIP is always a good start, then perhaps something unusual or something that affects the hip pocket (see Chapter 9).

You must also think long and hard about visuals. Television news crews are unlikely to take the time to attend if there is nothing visually appealing for them to film. Similarly, think of press photographers.

The content of the 'speech' part of the press conference should be available in press kits, together with backgrounders, photographs and press releases (see Chapter 10).

THE PERSON

Ideally, your spokesperson will be a VIP from your own organisation, or an external VIP that you know will be a major drawcard. VIP or not, you need to ensure that he or she can handle the media. A press conference has all the pressure of an interview and then some. Although this is a managed event (managed by you), you are still at the mercy of the media. They will have done their research, so you must see that the speaker is equally prepared with information and answers for all sorts of questions that might arise. Practice is the key to coping with this, with you playing the role of devil's advocate with the speaker. If you are the speaker, arrange a situation with someone else. Envisage the worst possible case and practise for that. If the press conference is

being held to defend the organisation, the speaker or interviewee should be the chief executive officer or the most
senior person.

THE EVENT

Keep an eye on what is happening in the news and perhaps
talk to a couple of news editors to ensure that it does not
clash with any other events in their news diaries. Try to give
the media about two weeks' advance notice of the press
conference so they can make a note of it in their diaries, but
do not forget to follow this up with a call a day or two
before the event. Supply journalists with a brief as part of
the initial invitation so they can conduct their own research.
Before lunch is the ideal time for a press conference for
broadcast and print journalists.

DURATION

A press conference can range in length from one minute to
an hour or longer. Generally, politicians are loath to give any
more than a 'doorstop' press conference, which is a press
conference while they are on the run (on the way from one
meeting to the next, getting in or out of their car at a
function). This can put you in a difficult situation, as the
journalists will then turn to you wanting answers. You may
want to give journalists a press release or statement at the
beginning of the press conference, but save the full press kits
until the end, or you will lose your audience before the
speaker even gets started. Do not forget to allow time after
the press conference for an in-house review and feedback
session. This will help for next time.

THE VENUE

A suitably sized meeting room or board room within your
own organisation is ideal from your point of view. It means

that all the last-minute preparation is happening on-site, which reduces logistical problems.

Make sure there is room for television crews (complete with cameras, lights and sound booms) as well as radio and print journalists. Particularly ensure that there is enough room for the television crews without restricting the access of all the other journalists. It is a common complaint that television journalists with their strength of numbers tend to push to the front, get what they want quickly, then push their way out again. Make sure that, whatever venue you choose, there is room for everyone to negotiate.

SPECIAL NEEDS

Apart from seating, you should take into account the other needs of the media:

- Is your venue easily reached by the media, or should you supply transport?
- Is there adequate seating in your venue?
- Are there enough phone lines, particularly for radio journalists, who may want to phone their copy back to make the noon bulletin?
- Is the sound system adequate? A high-quality sound system can be sourced directly (with sound source jacks) by the journalists with tape recorders, avoiding the clutter of microphones that sometimes cover the speaker's face.
- Have you provided adequate signage, and informed the reception desk to expect the media? Have you organised someone to help meet and greet the media as they arrive and to look after their needs?
- Have you arranged light refreshments (morning tea)? This will be appreciated and generally not misconstrued as a 'freebie' organised to obtain favourable coverage.
- Have you organised name tags? This tells you who has attended, and makes it easy to monitor their coverage. The remainder tags give you a list of names of people who

should have a press kit sent to them. Allocate someone to hand out tags and to mark off names at the door.

GETTING HELP

As with conferences and functions, sometimes it is better to spend that little extra for someone to take over the logistical side so that you can concentrate on the content. In the case of media conferences, most hotels, motels, resorts and restaurants have venues specifically designed for such an event. If you give them the numbers they can arrange all the seating, sound system, refreshments etc. Talk to other professional communicators who are in a similar situation about what to expect when organising a press conference. If you get on well with a news editor, you may also get some hints to ensure coverage. If you are working for a government department there is usually a set protocol and guide to follow as to who must be consulted and who should check material when, say, a minister is giving the press conference. This is also the case with many large organisations when the chief executive officer is the speaker.

CHECKLIST FOR PRESS CONFERENCES

☐ Can the information be covered in a press release?

If the answer is yes . . . *stop now.*

☐ Check the speaker's timetable.
☐ Check what is going on in the news and with news editors.
☐ Pick a time.
☐ If a government department, check procedures.
☐ Book a venue—check space, microphones, telephones etc.

☐ Alert the media.
☐ Prepare for questions.
☐ Organise visuals for television and photographs.
☐ Organise press kits.
☐ Phone-check for attendance.
☐ Reconfirm venue, press kits, refreshments, equipment etc.

FURTHER READING

Baskin, O. & Aronoff, C.E. 1988 (2nd edn). *Public Relations: The Profession and the Practice*. Wm C. Brown, Dubuque, IA.

16

Presentations

Presentations are used by organisations to convey information about a new product, service or concept to a small group of people. An array of methods is available to anyone having to make a presentation, and a mix of these can ensure an attentive and appreciative audience. Presentations usually include a visual demonstration or display.

BENEFITS

The major benefit of a presentation is that it is possible to present a large amount of new information to a specific audience, which can include practical demonstrations as opposed to more static speeches. Presentations are usually aimed at a select group, so feedback is instant.

DRAWBACKS

A presentation requires a lot of work, particularly at the research and preparation stages. The needs and interests of the audience should be anticipated, and time should go into achieving presentation methods as 'lively' as possible. Presenters must also have a good knowledge of the use of audiovisual aids and be able to present the information, and themselves, effectively. Presentations may require someone with considerable technical skill if they are demonstrating the use of a piece of equipment.

DELIVERY

It has been proven time and again by educational researchers that it is not a good idea to do a straight 'chalk and talk' (lecture) when making a presentation. People take in about 80 per cent of their information visually, about 11 per cent aurally, and the remainder through other senses such as touch and taste. This makes a strong argument for using a number of visual aids throughout the presentation. The choices include videos, slides, overhead transparencies, handouts, photographs and whiteboards. You need to know how to exploit these aids, though, as overuse or incorrect use can be worse than a straight talk. For instance, the maximum length for a video should be 10 minutes; and when using overhead transparencies, do not crowd the page (about 20 words is readable). The type you use should be at least twice the size of that from an ordinary typewriter.

Remember, the more senses that can be used in a presentation, generally the more effective the communication flow. For instance, if you involve not only sight and sound but also taste, smell and touch, you should reach all of your audience. The most important tip for a presenter, though, is to rehearse, rehearse, rehearse. Even then there is no guarantee that it will be all right on the night, but the odds will rise in proportion with the amount of preparation you have done.

CONTENT

When preparing a presentation, an educational learning theory called 'primacy and recency' comes in handy. Put simply, this is the 'first and last' theory: people remember what they hear and see at the start and at the end, but the middle is a bit of a blur. For the presenter this middle section is the 'danger' zone, and requires some thought when planning. Consider you are making a 10-minute presentation. You know that everyone is tuned in at the start and will revive at the end. If you can, start with a bang and finish with a similar bang to tie it all together.

Now to the danger zone. The best method for breaking up this grey zone is to build in lots of changes of pace. This could be as simple as telling a joke or as complicated as a computer visual display. Do not attempt the former if you (like me) cannot tell jokes. Do not use too many statistics or, if you do, simplify and illustrate using graphs, maps or graphics. If you know you have to present a lot of details, provide a handout.

Here is an example of a 10-minute presentation for a new sparkling wine, 'Sparkler'. The audience consists of wine merchants.

1. Start with a bang: pop the cork of 'Sparkler' and another brand.
2. Place side by side close to the audience. Ask the group to keep an eye on the contents of both bottles throughout the presentation.
3. Show an overhead transparency (OHT) of the logo on a large screen.
4. Talk about the difference between 'Sparkler' and other sparkling wines, while passing around the grapes used in this wine for participants to touch and taste.
5. Show an OHT with diagrams of the fermentation process to explain the technical difference.
6. Distribute handouts with a graph of the yeast quantities used in 'Sparkler' and various other brands while talking about the difference with 'Sparkler'.
7. Play a 60-second video of the main commercial television advertisement proposed for 'Sparkler', commenting

that 30-second and 15-second stings have also been produced.

8. Hand out information kits including sample print advertisements, press releases and stickers.
9. Finish with a bang. Draw everyone's attention back to the two bottles. Compare the still bubbling 'Sparkler' with the other, now flat bottle.
10. Pour for the participants. Drink. (Allow time for questions and feedback.)

Educational research has found that retention rates for information rise markedly if people are involved in the presentation in some way. Asking questions is a good method, but getting the audience to actually do something is even better. In the above demonstration the group is involved at a number of points—observing bottles, touching and tasting grapes, looking at handouts and drinking the wine.

THE PRESENTER

The person delivering the material is the key to the success or otherwise of the presentation. They must be armed with verbal skills, such as clarity of speech; a measured, but not too slow, delivery speed; and enthusiasm (which will come through in the tone of their voice). It is also essential that they do not read the presentation, as this is guaranteed to lose the audience. Small palm cards with key words or an overhead transparency with bullet points to be covered are two useful methods of delivering a more natural and direct talk.

But remember that statistic that 80 per cent of information is taken in visually. This means that 'body language' requires a lot of planning too. The presenter should be adept at using audiovisual aids as well as any equipment they may be demonstrating or presenting. Try to avoid the use of any aids that require you to turn your back on the audience (i.e. whiteboard), unless you are good at writing sideways quickly.

This applies also to blackboards, flip charts and any other aids that make you break contact with your group.

The presenter should be aware of key non-verbal techniques such as maintaining eye contact with the audience. This does not have to be a constant stare at each person in the group in turn, but the presenter should make some contact with every member of the group if numbers allow. If working with a large group, the presenter should turn and address each section of the room at some time.

GETTING HELP

It may seem a bit strange, but the teacher education section of a library is a good place to start when you are making a presentation. It is here that you will learn how people best take in information, how to use audiovisual aids, and other presentation tips. If you are constantly going to be called on to make presentations, it may be worth doing a short course of study (one to three days) on instructional skills. These courses are usually on offer at technical or polytechnic colleges.

CHECKLIST FOR PRESENTATIONS

☐ Determine the needs of your audience.
☐ Find a suitable room.
☐ Include a large percentage of visual material.
☐ Start and finish with a bang.
☐ Ensure that the pace changes to avoid the 'danger zone'.
☐ Rehearse to make sure that your verbal and non-verbal language is appropriate.
☐ Have you included group participation?
☐ Have you left time for questions and feedback?

FURTHER READING

McCarthy, P. and Hatcher, C. 1996. *Speaking Persuasively: Making the Most of Your Presentations.* Allen & Unwin, Sydney.

17

Speeches

There are many different types of speeches that you could be called on to write in political, financial, educational, community and other contexts, and each of these could have a different function or purpose and be directed at a different audience.

AUDIENCE

It is important to consider the purpose of the speech and the target audience together. Purpose and audience are dynamic variables: that is, they modify each other. Below are two examples of what we mean.

1. A politician is giving two speeches—one at a charity fund-raising, the other to sell a government policy to a group of party members. The difference in purpose and context translates to a difference in audiences, even though the speaker might be addressing exactly the same group of people. For a start, the first audience is likely

to be better disposed towards the speaker (after all, it is a charity function), and will probably turn up with a positive mindset (perhaps expecting to be entertained, or to hear a bipartisan message from the politician). They are probably more relaxed, tolerant and easy-going—completely different from the group that turns up to listen to the politician explain why they will be paying more in tax.

2. The politician who is addressing a mixed audience—the (quite well-off) party faithful and a group of impoverished pensioners protesting against tax increases—is also dealing with two different purposes. The speech to the party faithful might be nothing much more than an information session—when, where, how, and maybe a bit about why. The speech to the pensioners is something quite different: it is not simply to provide information, but an exercise in damage control ('You will derive benefits from this policy: the country will be better off, and so will you, eventually'), or in convincing the audience that the politician shares their concerns, and has been (or will be) arguing their case in cabinet.

It is impossible to overemphasise the importance, for a speech writer, of analysing your speaker's audience. You should give consideration to the following factors:

- What is the attitude of the audience likely to be, to both the speaker and the material? A popular or highly credible speaker is more likely to be able to deal with difficult or unpopular issues than a speaker who has to devote most of the allotted time to trying to build up a tenable relationship with the audience.

- What is the size of the audience? A smaller group opens up possibilities (making it easier for the speaker to personalise the speech), but carries potential problems (the occasion can become 'too' personalised: there is no escape from a small, hostile audience). A larger group probably requires a more formal approach, and the likelihood of different literacy levels across that audience means aiming at the lowest common denominator, which will bore or alienate some members.

- Speaking of literacy—what do we mean by the term? Literacy is normally understood as someone's ability to read and write, but here we use it to refer to someone's overall familiarity with or understanding of their culture. For instance, the party members who turn up to hear their local member speak every month are probably quite familiar with the party, its policies, its differences from other parties, its various faction fights and groupings: that is to say, they are probably politically literate, at least with regard to their party. The group of pensioners, on the other hand, knows nothing about the political, personal or ideological contexts that gave rise to these latest taxes, and are quite illiterate.

The literacy of your speaker's audience is an important factor in speech writing. Perhaps the two most important questions any speech writer can ask are 'What does the audience know?' and 'What do they need to know?'. Unless you can work those questions out, you risk wasting most of your speaker's time—not to mention alienating the audience either because they are being told what they already know, or because they have not been given the background or contextualising information they need to make sense of the speech.

RESEARCH AND CONSULTATION

There is a whole range of additional information you need to have before you start to research and write the speech. What age group is the speech aimed at? Is it predominantly a male or female audience? What is their socioeconomic status? Add this information to other practical details, such as the venue (its size, acoustics, seating capacity, distance from audience), time of day or night, and duration, and you have a much better chance of coming up with a speech that is effective and functional.

The other point you need to consider is the question of protocols. If you are writing a speech for a politician, for instance, there is a range of dos and don'ts, procedures and policies, that you need to be aware of. The same may be true of non-political institutions.

Getting this kind of information is vital, but the most important time you spend prior to writing is whatever time you can spare to consult the speaker. What does the speaker want the speech to do? What is it meant to achieve? We have made the point that the nature of the audience modifies the purpose of a speech. The speaker should be able to tell you about the audience, and how she or he wants to relate to them.

You and the speaker need to agree as to the point of the speech. But what if there is no point? What if our politician is required to give a speech to party members every month but does not have anything of significance to say? It is your job to come up with an angle that will work. If the information is boring or unlikely to excite or interest anyone, try to think of a way to recontextualise it so that it is meaningful to the audience.

Once you know what the purpose of the speech is, you need to familiarise yourself with the topic or area. There are obvious sources: the speaker, the library, newspapers and journals, and the Internet. Build up a file before you start writing, and when you are satisfied that you have enough information, select the material that most suits your speaker, your purpose, the duration of the speech, and the literacy of your audience.

Once you are ready to start, go back to the speaker and consult again. The speaker has to be confident that the material is suitable: after all, he or she will be required to defend the material and answer questions about it. Whenever you need to make a major decision about material, language, tone or mode of presentation, consult the speaker.

WRITTEN AND SPOKEN LANGUAGE

There are both differences and similarities when it comes to comparing written and spoken language. To start with the most obvious similarities:

- Both are normally oriented towards another person.
- Also, in order to communicate effectively with that person or persons, the language that is used and the messages or ideas that are being dealt with need to be carefully organised.

In other words, the idea—the stereotype, if you like—that written communication is highly formalised and organised, while spoken communication is spontaneous, is a myth. Both forms of communication are normally oriented towards an audience of some kind, in order to convince, denounce, inform, entertain, warn or praise.

While the conversations, jokes, interruptions, speeches, asides and exclamations that people indulge in seem spontaneous and unselfconscious, if you study them carefully these exchanges are usually carefully staged, timed and performed. In other words, there are a large number of (unwritten) rules which speakers must adhere to for their conversations and game-playing to seem natural and spontaneous.

It might seem strange that we need to 'perform' spontaneity, but anyone in the business of speech writing will be familiar with this apparent contradiction. There are a number of ways in which speech is said to be different from writing, and the most obvious of these—and in some ways the most valued of them as well—is that while writing is meant to be crafted, deliberate, formal and distanced, speech, we are supposed to believe, is natural and personal: it comes straight from the heart, and is therefore more likely to be truthful and sincere.

Speech writers know this, and usually try to take advantage of this greater credibility. Any person giving a speech—whether they be politician, company director, community leader or journalist—knows that people are more likely to listen to them, take what they say seriously, and respond appropriately, if they think the person giving the speech is truthful and sincere. They expect other things as well, such as information and expertise, but whether people accept the information you provide them with as being credible and relevant will often depend on how convincing your performance is.

We make the point here that there are significant differences between written and spoken communication, but what we have been suggesting is that these differences are based on the idea that speech is somehow more personalised and sincere than writing. And speech writing, which is a formalised and deliberate act of oral communication, usually attempts to make use of this personalised 'touch'.

The following are the main characteristics of speech that mark it as natural, sincere, spontaneous and personalised, and which differentiate it from writing:

- Speech usually makes far less use of language that is complex, polysyllabic, highly technical, allusive or ambiguous. Most of the words used should be short, non-technical, familiar to the audience and easily explicable: after all, an audience needs to take in what is being said very quickly.
- Sentences are shorter and less complex. A long, convoluted sentence will lose an audience because they are not sure what the point is, where the sentence is going, or what information is being communicated.
- Speech normally does not attempt to convey as many ideas as is the case with writing, and these ideas are usually communicated in a way that does not attempt to convey their full complexity.
- Speech is usually repetitive. That is, while only a few, straightforward ideas or bits of information are communicated, these are normally repeated consistently so the

audience will remember them, and understand their significance.

- Speech normally makes extensive use of examples and anecdotes, which gives an audience a base for ideas or information.
- Speech makes use of the personal pronoun 'I' to a much greater extent than does writing.
- Speech usually employs rhetorical devices (such as direct appeals to the audience). Speech also tends to make greater use of emotive language.

Textbooks will tell you that speech makes use of these characteristics because an audience does not have a text to refer to or does not have time to go over things and think them through, and this is perfectly true. But the other main reason speech—and in particular formalised speech—employs these characteristics is because they help to provide a convincing performance of spontaneity and sincerity.

In writing a speech, it is important to remember that the success of what is being communicated is tied up with the performance of the speaker and her or his ability to relate to and reach the audience.

WRITING THE SPEECH

You have researched and consulted, compiled a file and edited it, and you have distilled the information down to a few salient points. And you know that you have to use simple, straightforward language, short sentences, plenty of repetition, examples and anecdotes, and rhetorical devices. But how do you start writing?

The first thing to do is work out how many words you will need. Your speaker will not want to be getting through any more than 80 words a minute, and that could shrink to 70 a minute if this is meant to be an informal, cosy, intimate kind of speech. If your speaker has 30 minutes, then you have about 2000 words to play with—assuming, of course, that there is additional time for questions.

Numerous studies have indicated that audiences, no matter how interested, literate or well-intentioned, are unable to take in more than a few ideas at any one setting. In 30 minutes you might want to distil your material into two or three main ideas, and spend most of your time on examples, anecdotes and repetition.

Should you try and add some humour to the speech? This depends on a number of things:

- Is your speaker comfortable with humour? Humour that does not work will sap the speaker's confidence and alienate the audience.
- Is humour appropriate to the subject matter? A few years ago Alexander Downer, then leader of the federal Opposition in the Australian parliament, gave a speech during which he referred to the Opposition's policy on domestic violence as 'the things that batter' (a play on another policy catchphrase, 'the things that matter'). He never recovered politically.

You have two or three main ideas that need to be communicated, and 2000 words to do this in. You should divide the speech into an introduction, the main body, and a conclusion.

The introduction

The introduction is probably the most important part of the speech, because first impressions will largely determine how the audience responds to the speaker. There are two main points to remember:

1. The speaker needs to tell the audience what he or she is doing there, what their purpose is, and what main ideas or information they will be covering. In other words, the audience needs to know why it needs to listen, and where the speech will be going.

2. This is the speaker's chance to grab the audience's attention, so it should not be wasted: start with something punchy, arresting or personalised. For instance, if the speech is to the party faithful about a new tax policy, it might start by quoting an impressive and pertinent statistic ('Australia has the lowest level of indirect taxation in the world'). If the audience is made up of pensioners, an anecdote about a conversation with the Prime Minister on the speaker's concern as to how this policy will affect pensioners would be more relevant.

The body

The body of the speech is where you repeat main ideas or information through exemplification. Ideas and policies are fine, but people relate to examples—particularly everyday examples. The party faithful will be able to make more sense of the new tax if the speaker tells them what it will mean for the manager of a small business, while pensioners will want to know what impact it will have on prices of consumables. Every example should carry the ideas, information or argument forward a little, without moving off into another issue or area of discussion.

The conclusion

The conclusion is the last chance to remind the audience of main points. One of the best ways of doing this is to use rhetorical devices to 'bring home' to them what this new policy means to their lives. A most impressive device is to suggest a kind of partnership between speaker and audience—something like 'I have the responsibility of ensuring that this works, you need to help ensure that it does and to tell me what you think about it, and we need to do something if things aren't working'. It is appropriate to use the personal pronoun 'I' throughout a speech, but in the conclusion 'I' should give way to 'we' wherever possible.

CHECKLIST FOR SPEECHES

Once you have a draft of the speech, you should consult the speaker and rehearse. At this point you should make final decisions about language, humour, and whether your anecdotes and examples work. You should work off a checklist, which could include:

☐ Are there any problems with pronunciation?
☐ Is the speaker's speed of delivery appropriate? Are there moments that require a pause?
☐ Would the speech benefit from visual aids? If so, where? Be careful here, because visual aids should be employed only if essential. Nothing deflates a speech more than an inept or dysfunctional performance with a computer or overhead projector. And if the information provided is too interesting it can distract attention from the speaker.
☐ What questions are likely to be asked of the speaker? Try to work out responses in advance.

Remember, the secret to the successful performance of a speech is the extent to which the speaker has confidence in the material in front of him or her. The more you research, plan, consult on and rehearse the speech with your speaker, the greater the likelihood of a successful speech.

FURTHER READING

McCarthy, Patsy and Thatcher, Caroline 1996. *Speaking Persuasively.* Allen & Unwin, Sydney.

Pease, Allan and Garner, Alan 1985. *Talk Language: How to Use Conversation for Profit and Pleasure.* Camel Publishing, Sydney.

18

Tours

Tours are an effective way to show off your organisation, its operations, services or infrastructure. Tours can either be very good for your organisation or very bad—with the success or otherwise being totally reliant on the amount of preparation you put in. Tours are a promotional exercise. Even an educational tour—say, a school visiting your organisation—can either put you in a good light or produce such a negative image that it requires post-tour damage control. Generally tours are of existing institutions or attractions for educational or entertainment purposes, but they can be a pre-opening glimpse for the media or major sponsors.

BENEFITS

There is much to be gained by running tours of your organisation, area or attraction. It can mean greater community awareness, and perhaps acceptance. More tangibly, it can mean positive publicity leading to increased business, or that detractors, armed with more knowledge, become supporters.

Preparation and communication are essential to ensure that the tour, wherever it may be, flows smoothly for the participants as well as those along the tour route.

DRAWBACKS

Though giving the appearance of being a simple task, running a tour can be time-consuming, disruptive and plain hard work. Considerable time must be spent so that participants take away a positive image of your organisation or attraction, with minimum disruption to the workplace or site during the tour.

BEFORE THE TOUR

As with most forms of professional communication, you must know your audience. In the case of tours you need to know essentials such as group size, dates, times and contacts, as well as ages and interests. If you were running tours of, say, a newspaper, you would need a different 'spiel' or script for a primary school group from that for university students or members of the community. Be careful to pitch your talk at the right level, and beware of talking down to anybody.

Find out what the group would like to know and any particular areas of interest well before the tour. For instance, if you work for a newspaper and a group of primary school students are interested in the Internet and the computer section of the newspaper, you should incorporate this in the tour. Perhaps you could make it the highlight or an integral element of this particular tour. Without going too far down the road of running individualised tours, this could be one extra stop, or one substitute stop along the way.

SIZE

It is generally a good idea to restrict the size of the group, especially when dealing with busy workplaces, construction sites or hazardous terrain. About 10 participants is ideal, no matter what the age. In a tour group this size everyone can hear what you are saying, can easily ask questions and see any displays or demonstrations. A group of 10 is particularly good if you want your tour to be interactive. When the group is covering difficult terrain (i.e. inside a mine or on a construction site), smaller numbers will also mean fewer headaches for the tour leader, who is trying to keep the group safe and on the 'beaten track'.

PEOPLE

People in the workplace groan when they see tour groups coming through, as it generally means disruptions to their routine. In their eyes the worst thing is that they are rarely told the group will be coming, and it can be a shock to see a clutch of active 10-year-olds converging on their desk or workspace. The best advice for anyone responsible for organising tours is: communicate, communicate, communicate. Ensure that staff know what is going on and when. You may have to use several forms of communication to reach everyone: e-mail, newsletters, memos, maybe even a note attached to all payslips (guaranteed readership). All section heads or managers must first be contacted to ensure that times are convenient. They may also be involved in the actual tour, so this is essential. Then contact anyone and everyone who may be involved in or affected by the tour.

STRUCTURE

Conducting a tour is a little like giving a speech or presentation in terms of structure. There is an old adage: 'Tell 'em what you're going to tell 'em. Tell 'em. Tell 'em what you've told 'em'. It is a waste of time for all involved if you do not prepare the participants in some way for what they will be seeing and doing during the tour. You may even have a 'mud map' (a rough, hand-drawn map) and information sheet of the attractions or points of interest to hand out at the start.

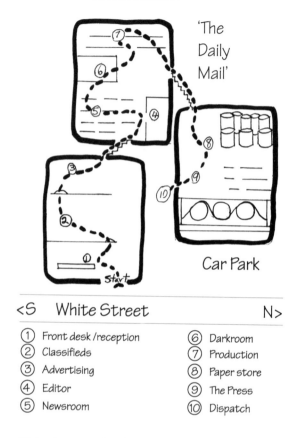

'The Daily Mail'

Car Park

<S   White Street   N>

① Front desk /reception   ⑥ Darkroom
② Classifieds   ⑦ Production
③ Advertising   ⑧ Paper store
④ Editor   ⑨ The Press
⑤ Newsroom   ⑩ Dispatch

Figure 18.1 An example of a 'mud map'

Figure 18.1 is an example of a 'mud map'. About one hour is a suitable length for a tour.

INTERACTION

If a tour is to be both enjoyable and educational, some sort of interaction should be included. It is commonly accepted that people remember more by 'experiential learning' or 'learning by doing' than just by listening and seeing.

This can be as simple as asking and inviting questions, or as involved as allowing tour participants to try their hand at a particular job or piece of equipment. For instance, a group touring a television station may get a chance to read the news using the autocue, or students interested in computers could search for the television station's homepage on the Internet. Interaction may be as simple and enjoyable as sampling the finished product at the end of a production line (i.e. in a chocolate factory).

Including some interaction or activity in your tour involves more time and coordination, but the pay-off will be in satisfaction for you and enjoyment for the participants. Some student groups even come equipped with a list of questions which have to be answered throughout the tour as part of their assessment. This is the teacher's way of ensuring some interaction, if it is not included in the tour.

SAFETY

Safety is a major consideration, particularly when you are touring areas with working machinery, such as printing presses at a newspaper. Electrical equipment with wires and cords, such as studio cameras at a television station, can also be a problem. With tourist attractions, the combination of animals and children can be the stuff of nightmares. If you have a tour group of young children it is highly recommended that teachers or parents form a large percentage of the group. Check with the safety officer for the particular area or department, and follow all their guidelines. Some tours, particularly those for the media, will be of areas under construction, and are generally hard-hat areas. Try to pick a time when work is not underway (e.g. during lunch), so you are not dodging jackhammers and live wires. Consult the foreman for the best days and times, and make sure you confirm your choice.

EVALUATION

All tours should be followed by some form of evaluation, preferably written. This feedback can be invaluable when modifying and improving the tour for future groups. Do not be afraid to invite criticism, as this is generally constructive. If you do not have an evaluation form it is worth the effort to create your own. This should be simple, non-time-consuming, and with space for extra comments (more feedback). Get people to fill in these evaluation forms before leaving. It is rare that anyone will go to the trouble of getting it back to you once they have left the site.

MEDIA TOURS

Tours for the media are common for organisations, usually prior to opening, to ensure advance publicity. The tour may be of a new hotel complex, tourist attraction or service. Media tours involve even more preparation in terms of providing information, as you want the media to have everything they may need to write a post-tour story. Generally, media kits are best and can include backgrounders, photographs and press releases (see Chapter 10). Journalists tend to be more cynical and world-weary than most tour participants, so make the tour newsworthy, and perhaps finish with something special to make it worth their time and effort. However, the post-tour attraction should not be too inviting. In one case, a media 'personality' decided he would skip the tour of the new hotel complex, but would definitely be there for lunch and drinks by the pool afterwards!

It is up to you to decide who will be on this tour, and it will be your responsibility to ensure a good turnout. Give lots of notice and lots of reminders (see Chapter 15).

GETTING HELP

Go on as many tours as you can to see how other people handle them. See what works and adapt the best ideas to your own program. Speak to other tour organisers about any problems they have encountered and any special ideas they may like to share.

CHECKLIST FOR TOURS

☐ Do you know the size of the group, age of partici-
  pants and contact person?
☐ Does the group have any particular interests or
  needs?
☐ Have you told all the section and department heads?
☐ Have you told everyone who might be involved in
  or affected by the tour?
☐ Do you have a map and information sheet?
☐ Is there some interaction included in the tour?
☐ Have you checked with safety personnel?
☐ Do you have an evaluation form prepared and ready
  to hand out? Have you allowed time for this to be
  completed at the end of the tour before the group
  leaves?

FURTHER READING

Baskin, O. & Aronoff, C. 1988 (2nd edn). *Public Relations: The Profession and the Practice.* Wm C. Brown, Dubuque, IA.

Index